W9-BZW-249

SLOVAKIA
in Pictures

Francesca Davis DiPiazza

Twenty-First Century Books

Contents

Lerner Publishing Group, Inc., realizes that current information and statistics quickly become out of date. To extend the usefulness of the Visual Geography Series, we developed www.vgsbooks.com, a website offering links to up-to-date information, as well as in-depth material, on a wide variety of subjects. All of the websites listed on www.vgsbooks.com have been carefully selected by researchers at Lerner Publishing Group, Inc. However, Lerner Publishing Group, Inc., is not responsible for the accuracy or suitability of the material on any website other than www.lernerbooks.com. It is recommended that students using the Internet be supervised by a parent or teacher. Links on www.vgsbooks.com will be regularly reviewed and updated as needed.

INTRODUCTION — 4

THE LAND — 8

▶ Topography. Rivers and Lakes. Flora and Fauna. Climate. Natural Resources. Environmental Issues. Cities.

HISTORY AND GOVERNMENT — 20

▶ Romans and Slavs. The Great Moravian Empire. The Magyar Occupation. Protest and Invasion. The Thirty Years' War. The Rise of Slovak Nationalism. Austria-Hungary and the Slovak National Revival. The New Republic. Slovakia Under Tiso. The Communist Regime. Prague Spring Reforms and Soviet Invasion. From Charter 77 to the Velvet Revolution. A New Slovakia. A New Era. Government.

THE PEOPLE — 38

▶ Health. Ethnic Groups. Language. Education. Religion. Lifestyles.

Website address: www.lernerbooks.com

Twenty-First Century Books
A division of Lerner Publishing Group, Inc.
241 First Avenue North
Minneapolis, MN 55401 U.S.A.

web enhanced @ www.vgsbooks.com

CULTURAL LIFE   48

► Literature. Art. Film. Music. Sports and Recreation. Holidays. Food.

THE ECONOMY   58

► Services, Tourism, and Trade. Industry and Manufacturing. Mining and Energy. Agriculture. Transportation. Communications. The Future.

FOR MORE INFORMATION

► Timeline	66
► Fast Facts	68
► Currency	68
► Flag	69
► National Anthem	69
► Famous People	70
► Sights to See	72
► Glossary	73
► Selected Bibliography	74
► Further Reading and Websites	76
► Index	78

Library of Congress Cataloging-in-Publication Data

DiPiazza, Francesca Davis, 1961–
   Slovakia in pictures / by Francesca Davis DiPiazza.
     p. cm. — (Visual geography series. Second series)
   Includes bibliographical references and index.
   ISBN 978-0-7613-4627-2 (lib. bdg. . alk. paper)
   1. Slovakia—Juvenile literature. 2. Slovakia—Pictorial works—Juvenile literature. 3. Slovakia—Geography—Juvenile literature. I. Title.
DB2711.D55 2011
943.73—dc22   2010000869

Manufactured in the United States of America
1 – BP – 7/15/10

INTRODUCTION

Slovakia is a country in the heart of central Europe. Forested mountains cross the land, and modern Slovakia has many beautiful wilderness areas and rural villages. Tourists come to ski and to hike through unspoiled countryside.

People lived in the region of Slovakia long before written history. Over the centuries, different groups moved into the region. The Slavs, ancestors of most modern Slovaks, arrived in the fifth century A.D. Under the Great Moravian Empire, which began in 833, Slovaks adopted Christianity. Hungarian invasions in 907 brought an end to the empire. For most of the next thousand years, Slovakia was part of the Kingdom of Hungary. The ruling classes, who were mostly Hungarian, owned large farm estates. They enjoyed many privileges and rights, such as voting. They denied these same rights to the farmworkers, who were mostly Slovaks.

In the 1800s, Slovaks began to develop and express pride in their own culture and language. Their rulers, however, kept tight control.

They allowed only the Hungarian language in Slovakian schools, for instance. Many Slovaks emigrated from Slovakia to other countries, especially the United States.

Hungary was defeated in World War I (1914–1918). This allowed the Slovak and neighboring Czech peoples to form the independent nation of Czechoslovakia.

After World War II (1939–1945), new leaders took over Czechoslovakia. They were closely tied to the Soviet Union (Russia and fourteen other republics). This powerful nation practiced Communism, a system in which the government controls economic and public life. Czechoslovakia set up a Communist government. It banned other political parties and restricted free speech.

During the 1950s, the government built huge factories in Czechoslovakia. Many Slovak farmers moved to the cities for new jobs. Despite a rising standard of living, many Slovaks wanted freedom from Communist control.

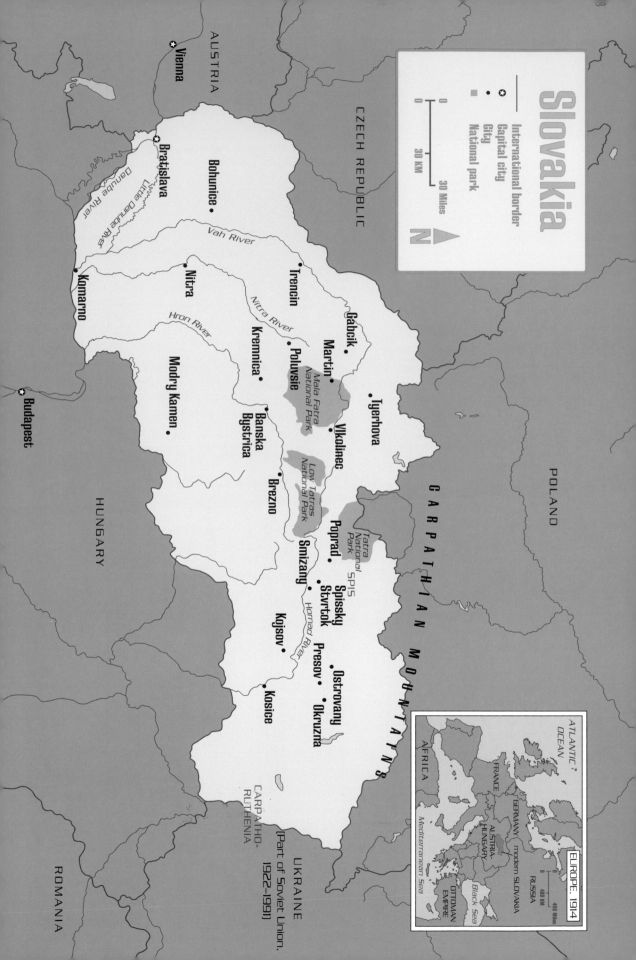

Slovakia

Legend:
- International border
- Capital city
- City
- National park

0 — 30 KM
0 — 30 Miles

N

AUSTRIA

CZECH REPUBLIC

✪ Vienna

✪ Bratislava

Bohunice •

Danube River

Little Danube River

Komarno ✪

Vah River

Nitra River

Nitra •

Trencin •

Hron River

Kremnica •

Poluvsie •

Martin •

Gabcik •

Tyerhova •

Mala Fatra National Park

Vlkolinec •

Modry Kamen •

Banska Bystrica •

Brezno •

Low Tatras National Park

Poprad •

Tatra National Park

SPIS

Smizang •

Spissky Stvrtok •

Kojsov •

Presov •

Ostrovany •

Okruzna •

Kosice •

✪ Budapest

HUNGARY

ROMANIA

POLAND

CARPATHIAN MOUNTAINS

CARPATHO-RUTHENIA
(Part of Soviet Union, 1922–1991)

UKRAINE

Homad River

EUROPE, 1914

ATLANTIC OCEAN

AFRICA

FRANCE

GERMANY

modern SLOVAKIA

AUSTRIA-HUNGARY

RUSSIA

OTTOMAN EMPIRE

Mediterranean Sea

Black Sea

0 — 400 KM
0 — 400 Miles

Czechoslovakia remained under strict one-party rule until 1989. In that year, a peaceful movement known as the Velvet Revolution brought down the Communist regime. After many disagreements, Slovaks and Czechs agreed to divide Czechoslovakia into two new nations—the Czech Republic and Slovakia. In 1993 Slovaks gained full independence.

Slovak prime minister Vladimir Meciar ruled his country with a strong hand, limiting democracy and human rights. In 1998 voters elected new leaders. The new prime minister, Mikulas Dzurinda, promised to strengthen democracy.

Geographers do not agree on the exact borders of Europe. According to some, however, the center of the continent is in Kremnica, Slovakia. A stone marks the spot in this old mining village.

In the twenty-first century, Dzurinda's government oversaw Slovakia's successful changeover to a modern economy. Minority ethnic groups gained greater rights after years of discrimination. In 2004 Slovaks elected Ivan Gasparovic as president. The same year, Slovakia became a member of the European Union (EU). This economic and political union of nations in Europe aims for peace, prosperity, and freedom.

In 2009 Slovakia began to use the euro, the shared currency of the EU. Being invited to join the "eurozone" was a sign that the country's economy was running well. Though unemployment remains a challenge, Slovakia's 5.4 million citizens look forward to better opportunities in the coming years.

 Visit www.vgsbooks.com for links to websites for up-to-date information about Slovakia's economy.

THE LAND

Slovakia is a small nation in central Europe. The mountainous country is landlocked, with no border along an ocean or large sea. Slovakia covers 18,932 square miles (49,033 square kilometers). It is about the size of West Virginia. Slovakia's neighbors include Poland to the north, Ukraine to the east, and Hungary to the south. Austria lies to the southwest and the Czech Republic to the northwest.

Topography

Snowcapped mountains, winding river valleys, and fertile plains are typical of Slovakia's topography, or landscape. Some parts of the country remain nearly untouched by human activity. Slovakia has two main regions—the Highlands and the Lowlands. Mountains and hills form the Highlands, running east and west across most of Slovakia. The mountains are the western end of the rugged Carpathian Mountains that stretch across central Europe.

The Male Karpaty Mountains rise near the Slovak capital of Bratislava, in the southwest. They run northward along the border

with the Czech Republic. To the east of these mountains are the Mala Fatra (Lesser Fatra) Mountains. The Vah River divides this steep ridge. Thickly forested valleys lie between the rocky peaks. Clear mountain lakes fill small basins within the range. In the large wilderness areas of the Vel'ka Fatra (Greater Fatra) and Nizke Tatry (Low Tatras) ranges, hikers may spot wild boars and some rare European bears.

The High Tatras are north of the Vah Valley, running along Slovakia's border with Poland. The High Tatras are Slovakia's most rugged and steepest mountains. Gerlach Peak is the highest point in Slovakia and in the Carpathian Mountains. It rises to 8,710 feet (2,655 meters) above sea level. Ancient glaciers—slow-moving sheets of ice—carved the small lakes, sheer rock walls, and steep canyons of this range. Tourists have visited resorts and health spas in the High Tatras since the 1800s.

South of the Vah River Valley are the Low Tatras. The mountains are part of the Low Tatras National Park, the nation's largest national

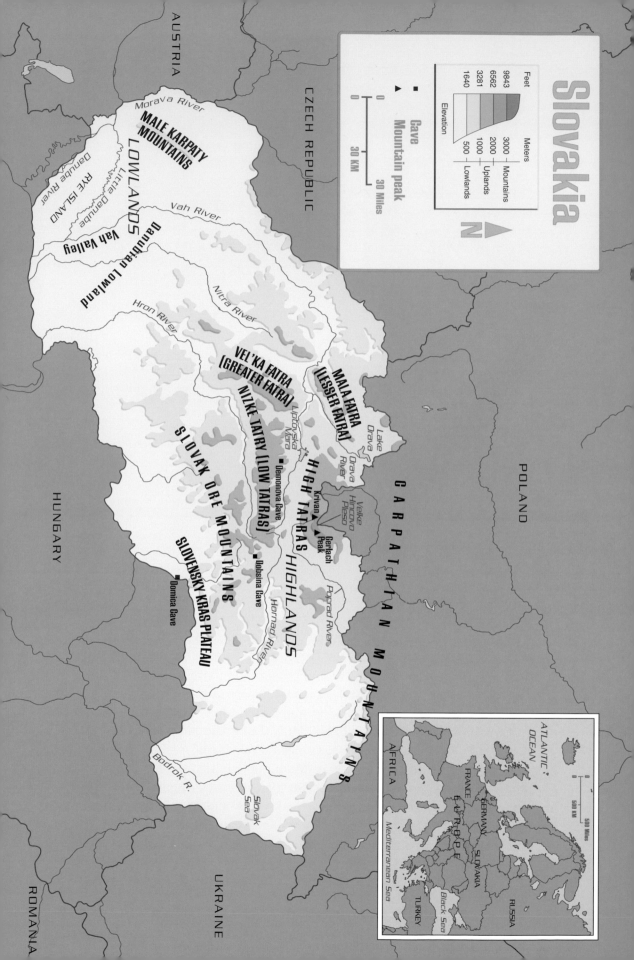

park. Many people visit the range to hike and ski.

The Slovak Ore Mountains stretch across central Slovakia into the Spis area, east of the High Tatras. The Spis towns are home to many ethnic Germans, who first settled in this region in the thirteenth century. Fast-flowing streams run southward from the mountains toward Hungary. The region includes the upper valleys of the Poprad and Hornad rivers. Small towns, farms, and villages dot the river valleys.

Krivan, a mountain in the High Tatras, has long been a symbol of Slovak pride. Considered the most beautiful peak in the land, it has been the subject of paintings and poems. And when Slovakia began using the euro in 2009, citizens voted for the mountain to be one of the images on their new money.

The Carpatho-Ruthenia area is on Slovakia's eastern border with Ukraine. There the Carpathian Mountains dwindle into rolling hills and small villages.

The Lowlands of south and southeastern Slovakia are part of a flat, dry plain that continues into Hungary. Near the southern border is the Slovensky Kras, a limestone plateau where water has carved narrow canyons and spectacular caves. An underground river runs through the 17-mile (27 km) Domica Cave, one of the longest caves in the world.

Limestone stalactites (mineral formations that form on the roof and sides of a cave) and clear pools of water adorn this section of the Domica Cave in the Slovensky Kras of southeastern Slovakia.

The Danube River runs along Slovakia's border with Austria and Hungary. The Slovak word for Danube is Dunaj.

The Danubian lowland is a fertile area in southwestern Slovakia. It is the country's most densely populated region. The low-lying plain stretches along the northern bank of the Danube. The capital city, Bratislava, is on the banks of the Danube. Marshes, pastures, and fields of grains and other crops cover the lowland's landscape.

Rivers and Lakes

Slovakia's rivers flow from the Carpathian Mountains and eventually empty into the Danube River. The river forms part of Slovakia's border with Austria and Hungary. It is the only river in Slovakia deep enough for big commercial ships. Other rivers provide irrigation water for farms and attract boaters, anglers, and tourists.

The Danube is Europe's second-largest river, after the Volga River in Russia. The Danube travels about 1,771 miles (2,850 km) from its source in Germany eastward to the Black Sea. For centuries the waterway has linked the nations of central Europe. The present-day river water is heavily polluted with waste from factories and cities that line its banks.

The Hron River is the second-longest river in Slovakia. It starts in the Low Tatras and flows southwestward to the Danube.

THE DANUBE FLOODS

Melting snow and heavy rains in springtime Slovakia sometimes combine with disastrous results. In 2006 swollen rivers overflowed their banks and flooded villages and fields. Workers placed 150,000 sandbags to control the flood, but the Danube River washed into parts of Bratislava. Hundreds of people fled rising waters, which led to two people's deaths.

The Morava River enters the Danube River just west of Bratislava. After passing the capital, the Danube divides into two channels. The main channel follows the Hungarian border. A smaller branch, known as the Little Danube, runs eastward and empties into the Vah River. Between the two channels lies Rye Island. It is the biggest river island in Europe.

The Vah River rises in the Vel'ka Fatra Mountains. It runs southward through western Slovakia. At the meeting of the Vah and the Danube sits the busy port of Komarno. It is the site of a vast shipbuilding and ship-repair complex.

The Nitra River flows southward toward the Danube from its source on the southern slopes of the Carpathians. The Hornad River passes the city of Kosice in eastern Slovakia. It then travels through the plains to the south.

Glaciers carved many mountain lakes in Slovakia. Velke Hincovo Pleso is the largest and deepest natural lake in Slovakia. It is a popular tourist lake. River dams have created artificial lakes too. The dams harness the power of rushing water to produce hydroelectricity. Lake Orava, in northern Slovakia, was created in 1954 by the damming of the Orava River. The Liptovska Mara is another artificial lake. It stretches along a plain just north of the Nizke Tatry Mountains. The Slovak Sea is a human-made lake in eastern Slovakia that is popular with vacationers.

Slovakia also has a large number of natural springs. Many of them are hot springs, warmed by heat rising from Earth's interior. Their soothing and healing qualities have attracted visitors for hundreds of years.

▶ Flora and Fauna

Forests cover almost 40 percent of Slovakia's land. In central and northern Slovakia, pine and spruce trees cover the higher slopes of the mountains. Forests of untouched beech trees grow in the east. Oak forests flourish in the south. Reeds and

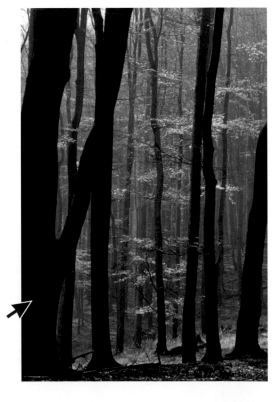

Beech trees are an important part of Slovakia's ecosystem. Beech trees can live for hundreds of years and grow up to 140 feet (42 m) tall.

ICE AGE ANIMALS

Several kinds of animals have lived in Slovakia since the last ice age, which ended ten thousand years ago. These species are called glacial relicts. The alpine newt, an amphibian, and the common lizard, a reptile, are glacial relicts. Relict birds include the common swift. Mammals are represented by the Tatra ground vole and the European snow vole. Voles are small rodents, similar to mice. Tiny freshwater shrimp called fairy shrimp survive in a lake in the Tatra Mountains.

marsh grasses thrive in the Danubian lowland. Southwestern Slovakia boasts the country's most fertile lowlands. White poppies blanket meadows there. Slovakia is also known for its many kinds of edible wild mushrooms. The linden, also called basswood, is the national tree of Slovakia. The tree's heart-shaped leaves provide shade. People brew its dried blossoms to make linden tea.

Many of Slovakia's forests have remained undeveloped by humans. They are home to some of Europe's most varied wildlife. The High Tatras shelter many species that are rare in Europe, such as brown bears. Predator mammals, which hunt other animals for food, include wolves, wild boars, lynxes, and wildcats. Forests are home to foxes, rabbits, and weasels. Otters, beavers, and muskrats live along rivers. Many kinds of bats inhabit Slovakia's many caves.

Marmots and chamois (a kind of antelope) both live in steep, rocky regions. The alpine marmot is the largest member of the squirrel family. It can weigh up to 17 pounds (8 kilograms). Goatlike chamois are known for their quickness and agility. Hunters prize the animals for their soft, valuable skins.

Slovakia's lands provide ample nesting places for birds. Pheasants, partridges, and several kinds of

The chamois is a goatlike animal native to the Tatra Mountains.

owls are common. The golden eagle, peregrine falcon, and common kestrel are birds of prey, or birds that hunt and eat other animals. Flocks of wild geese winter in the lowlands. Wild ducks, swans, gulls, and storks can be seen near rivers. The rare and protected great bustard is the biggest flying bird in Europe. It is endemic to Slovakia, meaning it lives only in that country, in the southern lowlands.

Amphibians in Slovakia include European tree frogs, Carpathian newts, and marsh tortoises. The adder is the only poisonous snake in the country. Perch, pike, trout, and carp are among the nation's many fish. Nearly three hundred kinds of butterflies and moths live in the nation. Honeybees also abound, and beekeeping has a long history in Slovakia.

◐ Climate

Slovakia's mountains greatly affect the nation's climate. During the summer, winds from the west bring rain to the ranges. The mountains shelter eastern and southern Slovakia from precipitation (rain and snow). As a result, the valleys and lowlands are warmer and drier than the mountains. The High Tatras get up to 70 inches (178 centimeters) of precipitation every year. Low-lying Bratislava, on the other hand, receives only 26 inches (66 cm) annually.

Summers in Slovakia are warm, with occasional heavy rain showers. Bratislava and Kosice average a temperature of 70°F (21°C) in July, the hottest month. Weather is changeable in the spring and fall. In these seasons, periods of warm, dry weather may follow days of chilly winds and heavy rain.

Winters in Slovakia are usually cold and cloudy. Snow covers the highlands from November to April. Kosice averages 26°F (–3°C) in January, the coldest month, while Bratislava averages 30°F (–1°C).

Occasionally, weather systems from the Mediterranean Sea, far to the south, affect Slovakia. Mediterranean winds sometimes bring hot weather and clear skies to Slovakia's lowlands. Much drier winds from the vast plains of Ukraine and Russia often blow through eastern Slovakia. Temperatures in the east are usually hotter in summer and colder in winter than in the rest of the country.

◐ Natural Resources

Slovakia's mineral deposits, rivers, forests, and fertile soil are its main natural resources. The Nitra River valley contains the country's richest deposits of coal. Near Kosice and in southern Slovakia, miners also extract manganese, an ingredient in steel production. Copper and iron ore exist in the Slovensky Kras region. Limestone and gravel pits supply the construction industry.

Grapes grow in this vineyard outside of Bratislava. Slovak farmers grow about eight varieties of wine grapes in the country's southern areas.

Small fields of natural gas and petroleum (crude oil) provide limited energy resources. River dams produce hydroelectric power. Uranium mining provides fuel for Slovakia's nuclear power plants.

The nation's forests provide wood. Farmers rely on the fertile soil and ample water of Slovakia's southwestern lowlands. Grains and livestock thrive there. On highland slopes, farmers cultivate wine grapes. Fruit and tobacco grow in river valleys.

◎ Environmental Issues

Slovakia struggles to control dangerous levels of air and water pollution. Mining and heavy industry, such as machinery-making factories, contaminate their surroundings with cancer-causing toxins. Air pollution from coal-burning plants is especially harmful to health. Toxins also fall to Earth in acid rain, which harms the nation's forests. Deforestation, or the cutting down of woodlands, threatens wildlife too.

Since joining the European Union in 2004, Slovakia has worked to meet the EU's environmental

TOO MUCH CARBON

Industries and machines that burn fossil fuels such as coal and gasoline send carbon dioxide (CO_2) into the atmosphere. The gas changes Earth's climate by trapping heat, like a glass roof traps heat in a greenhouse. A scientific report from the United Nations (UN) shows that the world's countries are producing twice the safe amount of "greenhouse" gases. Slovak industries create many times more CO_2 than that. Slovakia has pledged to reduce its greenhouse gas emissions but, like most countries has not yet met its goals.

laws and standards. Some factories began using less polluting fuels. The country has closed two nuclear power plants that did not meet EU safety standards. Several more nuclear plants operate safely. Their radioactive waste, however, is extremely dangerous.

Slovakia preserves many of its wilderness areas for science and research and for recreation. Nine national parks and fourteen regional reserves protect the nation's wealth of animals and plants. The Tatra National Park in the High Tatras covers 182,400 acres (73,815 hectares).

◉ Cities

About 56 percent of Slovakia's 5.4 million people are city dwellers. Hundreds of villages and towns with populations of less than 9,000 dot the countryside.

BRATISLAVA (population 428,000) is the capital of Slovakia and its largest city. It lies on the Danube River, near the borders of Austria and Hungary. People have lived on the site of the city since prehistoric times. Slavs settled there in the fifth century A.D. They named the city after a leader called Braslav.

Under Hungarian rule, Bratislava was known as Pozsony. The city became the headquarters of the Hungarian Diet (parliament, or legislature) in the 1500s. A bustling center of culture, education, and government, Bratislava attracted Slovaks, Hungarians, Roma, and Germans.

One of the city's most famous sites is its massive *hrad* (castle). Built in the ninth century, it overlooks the Danube. Another famous

The downtown Bratislava skyline includes the spire of the Cathedral of Saint Martin and, on the hill beyond the city, Bratislava Castle.

landmark is the fourteenth-century Cathedral of Saint Martin, in the city center. Many Hungarian kings were crowned in this church. In the Communist era, builders constructed large concrete apartment buildings around the city's edge.

Bratislava is an industrial center. The city's most important business is chemical manufacturing. Factories also produce textiles, refine oil, and process food. Cargo ships and passenger vessels use Bratislava's busy river port.

Visit www.vgsbooks.com for links to websites with additional information about Bratislava and other cities in Slovakia.

KOSICE (population 236,000) is Slovakia's second-largest city. It is the main city of eastern Slovakia, near the borders of Hungary, Ukraine, and Poland. Founded by German settlers in the thirteenth century, Kosice later became an important cultural center. After World War II, a giant new iron and steel plant near the city made Kosice an important industrial hub. But the factory has also caused extensive pollution in

Slovaks walk the historic streets of Kosice, the country's second-largest city.

the surrounding countryside. The city's residents are young, with an average age of thirty-five.

PRESOV (population 93,000), in eastern Slovakia, was settled by Slavs before A.D. 800. Slovakia's first printed book was printed at Presov in 1573. In modern times, the city has renovated many of its historical buildings. The root of the city's name comes from *eper*, which means "strawberry" in Hungarian. Strawberries do grow in the region, but industry is the main economic activity in Presov.

NITRA (population 88,000) spreads out around a castle on a hill overlooking the Nitra River, in western Slovakia. Prince Pribina founded Slovakia's first Christian church in Nitra in 833, though the building no longer remains. Soldiers of the Ottoman Empire, based in Turkey, attacked and destroyed much of the city in the 1600s. In modern times, students come to Nitra to study at the Agricultural University. The city also hosts an annual agriculture fair. Local industry includes chemical production and food processing. Vintners, or winemakers, produce a well-known wine from grapes grown on nearby hillsides.

BANSKA BYSTRICA (population 83,000) is on the Hron River in central Slovakia. Its name means "mining creek," and the city grew rapidly after copper, gold, and other valuable minerals were discovered there in the 1200s. German miners flocked to the town, which became one of the wealthiest in central Europe. But the mines have long been worked out. In World War II, the city was the seat of the Slovak National Uprising. A museum displays the story of this brave but unsuccessful uprising against Slovakia's pro-Nazi government in 1944. The modern city relies on industry and tourism for jobs and income. Its location amid beautiful mountains attracts tourists. Several ski resorts operate nearby.

SMIZANY (population 8,269) is Slovakia's largest village. German settlers established the village in 1242. It is in eastern Slovakia, at an elevation of 1,591 feet (485 m) above sea level. Small factories in the village include one that makes potato chips. Many visitors come to the scenic spot, near the entrance to the High Tatras National Park, and winter sports are popular in the village. The coach of Slovakia's national ice hockey team, Frantisek Hossa, is from Smizany.

HISTORY AND GOVERNMENT

Scientists have found remains of human ancestors in Slovakia from 270,000 years ago. The discovery of a little sculpture of a woman from about 25,000 years ago is evidence that people were active in Slovakia during the Stone Age. The sculpture is known as the Moravian Venus. An artist carved the 3-inch-long (7.6 cm) statue out of the tusk of a mammoth, an elephant-like prehistoric animal. Stone Age people of the time also made stone tools and weapons. They hunted wild animals and gathered plants for food. Their homes were temporary shelters in caves or simple huts.

After people in Europe began to farm in about 6000 B.C., groups began to settle permanently in the Danubian lowland. Prehistoric farmers cultivated small plots of grain. Over thousands of years, they tamed animals, fired pottery, and learned how to make tools and weapons from metal.

About 500 B.C., people called Celts spread from the west through central Europe, including Slovakia. The Celts were skillful iron- and metal-workers, and they cast the area's first coins. They set up towns and traded

goods with other peoples along the Danube. A Celtic group called the Boii built a town on the site of modern Bratislava. Here the Amber Road—a trade route between the Baltic Sea to the north and the Mediterranean Sea to the south—crossed the Danube River. From this location, the Boii carried on a busy trade in finely worked metal goods, weapons, and pottery.

The Boii settled in Slovakia, as well as in Moravia and Bohemia, parts of present-day Czech Republic. A Germanic tribe defeated the Boii in 12 B.C. and occupied many Celtic towns in Slovakia. Meanwhile, the Franks and other Germanic peoples moved into the Danube Valley. From their fortifications along the river, they staged raids on the armies of Rome to the south. The Roman Empire controlled much of southern Europe from its base in present-day Rome, Italy.

◉ Romans and Slavs

In the first century A.D., Roman troops arrived on the south bank of the Danube. Unable to conquer the Germanic tribes north of the river,

SAVED BY THE RAIN

In A.D. 172, the Roman emperor Marcus Aurelius led his troops against a Germanic tribe in Slovakia. During one battle, the Roman army was near defeat, due to heat and thirst. A sudden rainstorm refreshed them, and they went on to victory. Scenes of the so-called Rain Miracle appear on the Column of Marcus Aurelius, a memorial for the emperor in Rome, Italy.

the Romans built a series of strong-holds along the Danube. The river marked the northern frontier of the Roman Empire.

In the fourth century, people called Huns stormed into central Europe from the plains of central Asia. Under their leader, Attila, the Huns drove the Romans from the Danube Valley. Afterward, the Avars, another Asian people, con-quered Slovakia, Bohemia, and Moravia.

Thousands of Slavs followed the Avars into central Europe in the sixth century. The Slavic peoples eventually branched out into east-ern, southern, and western groups. They settled in small, circular villages known as *okruhlice*. The western Slavs included the Czechs (who settled in Bohemia and Moravia), the Poles (to the north), and the Slovaks.

In 623 these groups united their forces to drive the Avars from cen-tral Europe. The united group invited Samo, a merchant who headed a strong army, to lead them. After defeating the Avars, Samo and the Slavs were attacked by the Franks. At the Battle of Vogatisburg in 631, the Slavs emerged victorious. The victory allowed Samo to establish a Slavic state under his control. But Samo's realm quickly fell apart after his death in 658.

For two centuries after the death of Samo, Slovakia saw widespread violence and political chaos. Hostile armies crossed the region, while Slavic farms and cities declined or disappeared. Without a strong, cen-tral authority, Slavic princes ruled their small domains independently. Rival rulers fought for land and power.

The Great Moravian Empire

In 833 the Slavic prince Mojmir founded a new state in western Slovakia and Moravia called the Great Moravian Empire. The empire became one of the most important cultural, historical, and political milestones in Slovak history. It eventually controlled Bohemia as well as territory in what became Poland and Hungary. Bratislava and the town of Nitra grew as political and economic centers of the empire. In 833 Prince Pribina of Nitra founded the first Christian church in the area.

The Moravian ruler Prince Rastislav invited religious teachers from Constantinople (modern-day Istanbul, Turkey)—the center of the Eastern Orthodox branch of Christianity—to come and convert his people. The brothers Cyril and Methodius arrived in 863 to bring Christianity to the Slavs. They invented a new alphabet—called Cyrillic—to write Christian documents in local Slavic languages. Later rulers of the empire, however, preferred Roman Catholicism. They also replaced Cyrillic with the Latin alphabet, which the Catholic Church used. Most Slovaks became Catholic.

The Magyar Occupation

In the late ninth century, a huge force of Magyars—the ancestors of modern Hungarians—swept into the area from the south and the east. The Magyars defeated the Slavs at Bratislava in 906. The loss destroyed the Great Moravian Empire and led to the emergence of the Kingdom of Hungary. After the battle, the Magyars occupied cities and towns in Slovakia.

Slovak towns came under the rule of the Hungarian king, who was Catholic. Under Hungarian rule, few Slovaks rose to power. Hungarian landowners forced most Slovaks to become serfs—laborers who were attached by law, like property, to the large farming estates. Trade and mining in Slovakia benefited the Hungarian king and the nobles, who treated their serfs as slaves. Though they had no political power, Slovaks held on to their language and customs.

Many landowners built castles for protection. To strengthen eastern Slovakia, the Hungarian king invited Germans to settle in newly built towns in this region, including Kosice. Thousands of immigrants also came to mine gold, copper, and iron deposits in eastern and northern Slovakia. Slovak mines poured vast riches into the treasuries of Hungarian kings and princes. Trade along the Danube, productive farms, skilled artisans, and mineral resources made Slovakia an important economic center of Hungary.

Catholic reformer Jan Hus (standing, center) preaches to a crowd in this nineteenth-century line engraving. The Czech priest was convicted of heresy (spreading false beliefs) and was burned at the stake in 1415.

Protest and Invasion

In the late fourteenth century, a Czech priest named Jan Hus objected to the vast power and wealth of the Catholic Church. Hus's followers—called Hussites—demanded self-rule in religious and political affairs. The leaders of the church ordered Hus's execution in 1415. His death sparked a war in Bohemia. Thousands of Hussites fled to Slovakia.

In the early 1500s, inspired by Hus's ideas, the German priest Martin Luther tried to reform Catholicism. After the Church excommunicated (banned) him in 1521, he established the Lutheran Church. Followers of Luther, known as Protestants, found converts among Hungarians and Germans in Slovakia. Most ethnic Slovaks living in the countryside, however, remained Catholics.

At the same time, a new force threatened central Europe. Armies of the Ottoman Empire, based in Turkey, invaded the Hungarian kingdom. In 1526 Ottoman Turks conquered Buda, the Hungarian capital, and killed the Hungarian king in battle. The Turks then occupied Hungary as far north as the Danube River. That year, seeking protection, the people of western Hungary asked the Austrian king, Ferdinand, to be their king. He was a member of the powerful Habsburg dynasty (family of rulers). Ferdinand accepted, and Hungarian lands came under

Austrian Habsburg leadership. Even under Habsburg rule, however, Hungary still dominated Slovakia.

To escape further Ottoman attacks, in 1535 the Hungarian legislature moved from Buda to Bratislava. Slovakia remained unoccupied, while the Turks overran much of present-day Hungary.

The Thirty Years' War

In the early 1600s, Protestants in Habsburg lands struggled against the rule of the Catholic Habsburgs. In 1618 a rebellion against the Habsburgs in Prague—the capital of Bohemia (and of present-day Czech Republic)—touched off a wider war. The Thirty Years' War (1618–1648) was fought between Europe's Catholic and Protestant states. The Treaty of Westphalia finally ended the Thirty Years' War. Under Habsburg control again, many Hungarian nobles returned to the Catholic faith.

In the late seventeenth century, Habsburg forces defeated the Ottoman Turks at Vienna, Austria, the Habsburg capital. This victory freed much of Hungary from Turkish rule. In 1711 the old boundaries of the Kingdom of Hungary were restored.

For generations, most ethnic Slovaks had had no political rights. Slovak religious leaders made up a small, educated class. Most Slovaks, however, lived in poverty. Hungarian laws required them to pay taxes and serve in the military. Rural Slovaks inhabited rough

THE BLOOD COUNTESS

Elizabeth Bathory (1560–1614) was a Hungarian countess who lived her adult life in a castle in western Slovakia, then part of the Kingdom of Hungary. She is famous as one of the deadliest female serial killers in history. With the help of four servants, she supposedly tortured and murdered hundreds of young women. Legend named her the Blood Countess and claimed— falsely—that she bathed in her victims' blood. In 1610 she was arrested and imprisoned in a set of castle rooms. She was found dead there, four years later. Some claim that Bathory *(below)* was the innocent victim of lies told for political reasons, because she was a member of a powerful family the Habsburgs did not like.

dwellings and worked for low wages—if any—for the landowners. These hardships led to the rise of Slovak nationalism, the movement for self-rule.

The Rise of Slovak Nationalism

Empress Maria Theresa inherited the throne of the Habsburg Empire in 1740. She introduced sweeping changes in the forty years of her reign. These included schools for Slovak children and more rights for serfs. While Hungarian landowners resented their loss of power, Slovak nationalists in Bratislava took the opportunity to found the first Slovak newspapers. Maria Theresa's son Joseph II came to power in 1780 and abolished serfdom in his realm.

In 1848 rebellions swept through the capitals of Europe. Revolutionaries demanded forms of government that gave more power to the people. Slovak nationalists held a Slavic Congress with other activists in Prague. They discussed ways to gain self-rule and civil liberties, such as voting rights. But the Habsburgs ignored the demands of the congress.

In the same year, Ludovit Stur founded the Slovak National Council with other Slovak nationalists. Stur was a Slovak member of the Hungarian Diet (law-making body). The council asked the Diet for the right to form local Slovak assemblies. The Slovaks also wanted to use their own language in schools. Hungarian politicians, however, saw Slovakia as Hungarian territory and strongly opposed these steps.

Maria Theresa (left), empress of the Habsburg Empire, ruled over Austria, Hungary, Slovakia, and Bohemia from 1740 to 1780. **A plaque of Ludovit Stur (right)** honors the leader of the Slovak National Revival.

When the Diet rejected the Slovak petitions, fighting broke out in Slovakia. Hungarian forces soon put down the uprising and executed several rebels and their leaders.

Austria-Hungary and the Slovak National Revival

During the 1860s, Austria suffered military defeats in Italy and Germany. Continuing rebellion among the Slovaks and Hungarians also weakened the realm. In 1867, to keep Austria together, the Habsburg emperor Franz Joseph agreed to form a new state. It was called Austria Hungary, also known as the Austro-Hungarian Empire. One emperor ruled both Austria and Hungary, but the two parts of the empire controlled their own lands.

Hungarian leaders were determined to keep Slovakia under their control. They started a campaign of "Magyarization," named after the Hungarian ancestors, the Magyars. Under this campaign, Hungarian became the only official language in Slovakia. All Slovak schools in the region were closed. Only landowners—mostly a small group of Hungarians—could vote.

This policy and the continued poverty of their homeland drove thousands of Slovaks to emigrate from Slovakia to other lands. Over the next fifty years, about 20 percent of Slovaks left their homeland, many moving to the United States. Those who remained were mostly poor farmers and factory workers.

Slovaks had almost no political power. In this discouraging setting, however, some writers, teachers, and religious leaders—including Ludovit Stur—began the Slovak National Revival. They wanted to encourage pride in their distinct language, history, and cultural traditions. The Slovak nationalists formed groups and started magazines and newspapers. In them, they could express themselves in their own language. Slovaks living in other countries, especially the United States, supported the revival with money and ideas. Czech nationalists, who wanted self-rule too, encouraged the Slovaks.

NEW LIFE FOR AN OLD GODDESS

Women and working-class people played an active role in developing Slovak nationalism. A women's organization named Zivena formed in 1869. Zivena is the name of a life-giving goddess in old Slavic mythology. Elena Marothy Soltesova became one of the leaders of the group and of the Slovak movement for women's rights.

The New Republic

In 1914 an ethnic Serb assassinated the Habsburg heir to the throne of Austria-Hungary. War soon broke out between Austria and Serbia, an independent Slavic nation. Germany sided with Austria-Hungary. Russia allied with Serbia, setting the stage for World War I.

The Czechs and the Slovaks were still under Habsburg rule. They didn't want to fight against Russians and Serbians, however, who were fellow Slavs. Many Slovaks deserted the Austrian army to form the Czechoslovak Legion. This unit fought alongside the Russians until 1917. That year Russian revolutionaries overthrew the Russian government and took Russia out of the war.

Milan Stefanik

During the war, Slovak leader Milan Stefanik joined with Czech nationalists Tomas Masaryk and Eduard Benes. They set up the Czechoslovak National Council, which declared the founding of Czechoslovakia in the fall of 1918. The new republic included Slovakia, Ruthenia, Moravia, and Bohemia. Masaryk pledged that Slovaks would rule themselves within the new country.

World War I ended in November 1918, when Germany and its allies surrendered. The Austro-Hungarian Empire collapsed, and Hungary won its independence.

At the same time, a civil war was raging in Russia. Communist revolutionaries battled supporters of the Russian czar, or emperor. Eventually the revolutionaries won. They established the Soviet Union, a country that included Russia, Ukraine, and a number of other republics. The government followed Communist ideals, taking control of the nation's economy and all public life. Strict government control was meant to ensure that all citizens got a fair share of the nation's wealth. In reality, it led to harsh limits on personal and political freedoms.

Czechoslovakia's new legislature elected Tomas Masaryk president of the new nation. The first Czech-Slovak union brought advancement to Slovaks in many spheres of life—economic, educational, and cultural. Despite Masaryk's promises during the war, however, Czechs held most of the power and few government positions went to Slovaks. The Czech part of the nation was also richer and more industrialized than Slovakia. The government spent little money to develop Slovakia.

Many Slovaks felt betrayed. They continued to press for a nation of their own. A Slovak Catholic priest, Andrej Hlinka, led a new movement for self-rule. Hlinka founded the Slovak People's Party, which became the most active political group in Slovakia.

Slovakia Under Tiso

In 1933 Germans elected Adolf Hitler as their leader, but he quickly became a dictator (ruler with absolute power). Meanwhile, nationalists in the Slovak People's Party demanded separation from Czechoslovakia. They wanted closer ties with Germany. After Hlinka's death in 1938, his follower Josef Tiso became the head of the Slovak People's Party. He openly connected his political group with Germany's Nazi Party and pushed for Slovakia's independence.

Hitler demanded that Sudetenland—a part of Czechoslovakia settled by Germans—become part of Germany. Seeking to avoid another world war, French and British leaders met his demands, and Czechoslovakia lost one-third of its land. One month later, Germany's ally Hungary seized parts of southern Slovakia. Most of Slovakia's ethnic Hungarians lived in the south.

Hitler and his government promised Tiso that they would support him if he separated Slovakia from Czechoslovakia. In March 1939, Slovakia declared independence, calling itself the Slovak Republic. Tiso, the president, took orders from Germany. Like Hitler, he ran the country along fascist lines. (Fascism is a political system, run by a dictator.) Meanwhile, Nazi troops occupied Bohemia and Moravia. Czechoslovakia ceased to exist as a country.

In September 1939, Nazi Germany's invasion of Poland began World War II. During the war, German troops were stationed in Slovakia.

Josef Tiso (left) met with German leader Adolf Hitler (right) in March 1939. Six months later, Germany invaded Poland to start World War II.

These soldiers were part of the underground (secret) forces within the Slovak army who worked to rebel against Slovakia's ally Germany in World War II.

Factories in the region made weapons for the German armies. Slovak troops fought alongside Germany's forces. The Slovak government cooperated with Germany to send more than half of Slovakia's 130,000 Jews to concentration camps. Workers in the camps systematically murdered Jews and other prisoners. The Slovak government also imprisoned many Roma (formerly called Gypsies) in labor camps.

Some democratic and Communist Slovak leaders formed a resistance movement. Rebels tried to weaken the regime. They destroyed machinery in factories, stole fuel, and blew up ammunition.

Hitler's armies occupied most of central Europe. But as the war went on, Slovaks began to turn on Germans in greater numbers. Slovak units in German armies mutinied, or rebelled. In Slovakia's mountains, armed bands formed to fight for independence. On August 29, 1944, rebels began the Slovak National Uprising against the German-controlled Tiso government. It took Hitler's forces two months to crush the Slovak fighters.

Meanwhile, Soviet armies, which were fighting against Germany, were advancing rapidly into central Europe. Soviet forces liberated Slovakia by May 1945, when Germany surrendered.

The Communist Regime

After the war, Czechoslovakia reunited. Tiso and other members of the Slovak government were put on trial in Bratislava. The court sentenced Tiso to death by hanging.

New president Eduard Benes tried to preserve democratic, multi-party rule in Czechoslovakia. But by then, Soviet forces were overtaking many eastern and central European countries. In 1948 the Czech

Communists, with Soviet support, took over the government in Prague. The government nationalized, or took over, privately owned Czech and Slovak factories, businesses, and farms. The Communist Party also ran the media and the education system. Authorities jailed or executed people who spoke out against the changes. Many opponents of the regime were Slovak nationalists. Slovaks resented that Czechs continued to hold more economic and political power in the union.

Although technically Czechoslovakia was an independent country, in reality the Soviet Union controlled it. The new Communist governments of central and Eastern Europe were all under tight Soviet control. Together they were known as the Eastern bloc countries.

After World War II, the United States and the Soviet Union had become the world's two superpowers. Tension between the two was high. Although they didn't directly fight a war, their rivalry was called the Cold War (1945–1991). The West (the United States and non-Communist European nations) feared the growing Soviet power and the spread of Communism.

In 1949 the West formed a military alliance called the North Atlantic Treaty Organization (NATO). Its main purpose was to prevent a Soviet attack on Western Europe. Soviet leaders in turn formed the Warsaw Pact, a military alliance of Eastern bloc nations, including Czechoslovakia.

Czechoslovakia followed the Soviet economic model. The government set wages and prices and banned private ownership of large businesses and farms. The government forced farmers to work on state-run farms. More and more Slovaks became factory workers in cities.

A couple harvests cabbages on a state-run farm in Czechoslovakia. Under Communist rule, people were forced to work for government-run farms and industries.

Czechoslovakia's economy grew rapidly at first. But the central planning of the economy also caused waste and inefficiency. Fixed wages and lack of choices gave workers little incentive to work hard. The government had little money to spend on new plants and modern machinery. Factories gradually became outdated.

By the 1960s, the nation's economy was at a standstill. Factories and farms could not produce enough food and goods to meet the nation's needs. Shortages of food and consumer goods caused growing unhappiness with the government. The government allowed no public criticism of its policies. But some members of the Communist Party saw the need for economic political reform.

Prague Spring Reforms and Soviet Invasion

The reform movement gathered strength in the mid-1960s. Alexander Dubcek was a member of the Communist Party of Slovakia who wanted to reform the system. He led a movement for more freedoms and rights, seeking to create "socialism with a human face." (Socialism is a less extreme form of Communism.) For instance, Dubcek wanted to let individuals own small businesses.

In January 1968, party members elected Dubcek secretary-general (head) of the Communist Party of Czechoslovakia. He was the first Slovak to hold this powerful post. Under Dubcek, the party lifted state control of the media and proposed democratic elections.

This time of reform and the hopeful mood it inspired in Czechoslovakia was called the Prague Spring. But leaders of other Warsaw Pact countries feared they would lose their power if their own citizens demanded such changes.

Acting on these fears, the Soviet Union and several of its allies invaded Czechoslovakia on August 20, 1968. The Soviets arrested Dubcek and other pro-reform leaders. Angry citizens confronted Soviet tanks on the streets of Prague, Bratislava, and other cities.

Alexander Dubcek was a Communist. But he wanted to give the people of Czechoslovakia more independence from the government. He eliminated censorship and gave citizens the right to speak out against the government.

Afterward, a pro-Soviet Czech government put an end to most of Dubcek's reforms. Powerless to stop this, a large wave of emigrants left their country.

The next year, Gustav Husak became the new head of the Communist Party of Czechoslovakia. Under Husak, the party got rid of many remaining pro-reform leaders and increased censorship.

From Charter 77 to the Velvet Revolution

The Husak regime was unable to bring prosperity to the nation. People remained discontented. More and more, the nation's writers, artists, and thinkers began to call for free expression. In 1977 many of these activists signed a document—called Charter 77—demanding an end to censorship. The document also became a rallying point for those who wanted free, open elections and a multiparty state. One of the leading voices for change was the Czech writer Vaclav Havel.

The Soviet Union was also struggling with a poor economy and unhappy citizens. In the mid-1980s, Soviet leader Mikhail Gorbachev moved to make his country more democratic. He called for a more open society. Gorbachev's concept of openness, called glasnost, affected the other countries of the Warsaw Pact. Their Communist leaders, including Husak, faced growing demands for similar reforms from their citizens.

The end of Communist control in Czechoslovakia came swiftly. Because it was smooth and peaceful, it became known as the Velvet Revolution. Antigovernment demonstrations in 1988 marking the twentieth anniversary of the Soviet invasion of Czechoslovakia grew into a powerful movement. In 1989 demonstrations in Prague forced Husak and the Communist government to resign. Vaclav Havel became the new president of Czechoslovakia.

Czechoslovakia was not alone in overturning its Soviet-style Communist government. Every other nation in the Eastern bloc did the same in 1989.

THE TOSS OF A COIN

After the crackdown on freedoms in 1968, Communist rulers in Czechoslovakia were afraid criticism of the regime could lead to another rebellion. They tried harder to control all public speech. For instance, clergy couldn't give sermons about political topics, such as the nation's high divorce rate. If clergy disobeyed, they lost their licenses to work. Sometimes government decisions made no sense. For instance, officials banned a song that featured a boyfriend saying he would flip a coin to see if his girlfriend loved him. Censors claimed the words insulted the government's money.

Czechoslovakia's elections in the summer of 1990 brought the Slovak opposition movement Public Against Violence to power in the National Assembly. Vladimir Meciar, one of the movement's leaders, became the Slovak prime minister.

Unlike Czech leaders, Slovak politicians, including Meciar, opposed rapid change. They feared that loss of government control would cause widespread unemployment and inflation (rising prices). Meciar and many other Slovaks also supported the creation of a separate Slovakia.

In 1991 the fifteen republics of the Soviet Union officially became independent. On December 25, the Soviet Union ceased to exist.

In Czechoslovakia, Meciar founded the Movement for a Democratic Slovakia (MDS) to work for Slovakia's independence. In the national elections of June 1992, members of the MDS won a majority of seats in the Slovak legislature.

By 1992 the debate between Czechs and Slovaks over what direction the country's economy should take had grown bitter. As a result of that, the National Assembly agreed to split Czechoslovakia into two separate countries.

A New Slovakia

On January 1, 1993, Slovakia became a free and independent country. Bohemia and Moravia together formed the new Czech Republic. Slovaks celebrated the triumph of Slovak nationalism.

The celebratory mood did not last long, however. Meciar soon showed he was not committed to full democracy. His government stepped up control over the press and television. It also stripped away the rights of minorities in Slovakia. For instance, it restricted the right of the Hungarian minority to use the Hungarian language. The Roma population continued to suffer from discrimination and high unemployment rates, as it had for centuries.

Under Meciar, corruption was high, with government and busi-

A border guard disposes of the Czechoslovakian border sign after the Czech Republic and Slovakia officially became two separate countries in 1993.

ness leaders accepting bribes and giving special favors to friends and allies. Meciar continued Slovakia's ties with Russia, the seat of the former Soviet Union. But Slovakia's relations with its neighbors the Czech Republic and Hungary were poor.

Visit www.vgsbooks.com for links to websites with additional information about Slovakia's independence.

◎ A New Era

In 1998 Slovakians rejected Meciar's rule. They voted in politicians who promised to work together to promote democracy, modernization, and good relations with the rest of the world. New prime minister Mikulas Dzurinda led a new government that introduced reforms.

Dzurinda and the legislature worked to create a healthy democracy in Slovakia. They made changes to the constitution to create a fair justice system. The government continued good relations with the east but also turned toward western Europe. Slovakia wanted to join NATO and the European Union. The EU is a community of democratic nations in Europe. Member nations must meet standards of economic and social health. Slovakia worked to improve rights for minorities, including the Roma.

Most Roma continued to struggle with prejudice and poverty. In 2000 Slovak racists brutally murdered a fifty-year-old Roma woman named Anastazia Balazova. The murder shocked the nation and proved the need to improve ethnic relations. Politicians called for better treatment and opportunities for Roma.

A Roma family plays cards together at home. Most Roma in Slovakia live in poor conditions due to racism that makes it difficult to find employment.

Slovaks elected Ivan Gasparovic president in 2004 and again in 2009. Under his administration, Slovakia adopted the euro as its official currency.

In 2003 a majority of Slovak citizens voted for EU membership. Dzurinda noted proudly that this was the first time in history Slovakia was truly free to decide its own path. Also in 2003, the government of Slovakia supported the U.S.-led war in Iraq to remove dictator Saddam Hussein. The country sent a small number of troops to Iraq, an unpopular move among rank-and-file Slovaks.

Slovakia officially joined the EU and NATO in 2004. That year Ivan Gasparovic won the presidential election. Robert Fico replaced Dzurinda as prime minister after legislative elections in 2006. Fico had earlier served on committees to promote the rights of women and minorities. He made the popular decision to withdraw Slovakia's troops from Iraq by the end of 2007.

In 2009 President Gasparovic won reelection and Slovakia became the first former Warsaw Pact country to replace its currency with the euro. Nations in the euro-zone must have healthy and secure

TRAGEDY AND LUCK

Slovakia's deadliest airplane crash occurred on January 19, 2006. A Slovak military plane carrying forty-three people crashed and burned in a Hungarian forest. The passengers were Slovak peacekeepers returning home from a tour of duty in the troubled region of Kosovo in Serbia. Rescue crews on the bitterly cold night were amazed to find a soldier wounded but alive among the wreckage. They reported that his survival was pure luck: he was in the plane's bathroom, which was not badly damaged.

economies. The adoption of the euro showed how far Slovakia had come as an independent nation and was a sign of hope for the future.

▶ Government

Slovakia adopted its constitution on January 1, 1993, when it separated from Czechoslovakia. All citizens eighteen years and older are eligible to vote.

The executive branch is made up of a president, a prime minister, and a cabinet of ministers. The ministers oversee government departments of justice, education, finance, and so forth. Voters elect the president to a five-year term, with a limit of two terms. The president's job is mostly ceremonial. The president appoints the prime minister, who holds a far more powerful position. The prime minister is usually the leader of the party that wins the most seats in Slovakia's legislature. With the advice of the prime minister, the president also appoints the cabinet.

The National Council is Slovakia's legislative branch. The council passes laws and amendments to the constitution. Voters elect 150 representatives from many different political parties to four-year terms. Because there are so many parties, no one has a large majority. Small parties often form coalitions with other like-minded parties.

The highest court of the judicial branch is the Supreme Court. The legislature elects judges to this court. The president appoints judges to a constitutional court, which decides important questions of law. District courts and county courts hear cases at the local level.

Slovakia is divided into eight administrative regions, including the capital city of Bratislava. The country also has seventy-nine smaller districts known as *okresy*. Citizens vote for mayors and local officials.

As a member of the European Union, Slovakia sends 14 representatives to be among the 785 members of the European Parliament, the EU legislature. The parliament meets in two places, one in France and one in Belgium.

THE PEOPLE

Over thousands of years in Slovakia, farming communities developed in isolated mountain valleys and in the lowlands of the southwest. In modern times, industrialization drew many rural people to cities for work. But still only 56 percent of the nation's 5.4 million inhabitants live in urban areas. The average for Europe as a whole is 75 percent. In the Czech Republic, for instance, 77 percent of the people live in cities.

Overall, Slovakia's population density stands at 285 persons per square mile (110 per sq. km). This is lower than the Czech Republic's 337 persons per square mile (130 per sq. km) but about the same as Hungary's and Austria's population densities. The areas around the High Tatras and Carpatho-Ruthenia are home to the fewest people. Fertile land and big cities in the southwestern lowlands can support more people. This is Slovakia's most densely populated region.

Slovakia's population is falling. The fertility rate is 1.2 births per woman. This is one of the lowest birthrates in the world. Slovakia's

government is concerned about the country's low birthrate. If Slovakia's rate continues, the nation's population will fall to 5.2 million by 2025 and to 4.7 million by 2050.

Health

Slovakia's constitution guarantees free basic health care for everyone, but this has proved expensive to provide. The government has gradually turned over its state-run health-care system, created during the Communist era, to private owners. The goal is to increase effectiveness and reduce costs. Under the newer system, patients pay for certain services.

Slovakia's health statistics are good overall. Almost everyone has access to doctors, though medical facilities are not always as advanced as in western Europe. The country's good sanitation systems and widespread immunizations (shots given to prevent disease) keep certain diseases under control. Slovakia's rate of HIV/AIDS infections (human

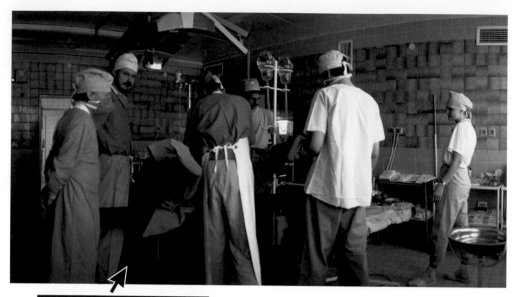

Surgeons perform a surgery in a hospital in Bratislava. Heart disease and cancer are among the leading causes of death in Slovakia.

immunodeficiency virus/acquired immunodeficiency syndrome) is 0.1 percent of the adult population, among the lowest in the world.

The infant mortality rate (IMR) is one indicator of a country's health standards. The IMR reflects the number of babies who die before their first birthday. Slovakia's IMR is 6 deaths out of every 1,000 live births. This is about average for Europe, but the Czech Republic's IMR is lower, with only 4 infant deaths per 1,000 births.

Average life expectancy in Slovakia is 74 years. Males can expect to live about 70 years, while women's life expectancy is 78. In Europe overall, the average life expectancy is 75 years.

Slovaks face the same health risks as people in other industrialized nations, such as heart attacks and cancer. Unhealthy lifestyles such as lack of exercise, unhealthy diet, smoking, and poor stress management represent the major health problems in Slovakia. About 40 percent of adults smoke cigarettes, and lung cancer rates are high. High levels of environmental pollution, which can cause cancer and other illnesses, are another concern throughout the country.

Ethnic Groups

Several different ethnic groups settled in Slovakia during its long history. In the twenty-first century, ethnic Slovaks make up 86 percent of the population. They are the descendants of the Slavs who first migrated into central Europe in the sixth century. Although they are both Slavic peoples, Czechs and Slovaks developed separate cultures. Slovakia's language, writing, music, and food all differ from the Czechs'.

Hungary's control over Slovakia ended after World War I. Some conflict still remains in Slovakia, however, between ethnic Slovaks and ethnic Hungarians, who are descendants of the Magyars. Ethnic Hungarians account for about 9 percent of Slovakia's population. Mostly living in southern Slovakia, they make up a majority in the areas near the Danube River and the Hungarian border.

Often Hungarians in Slovakia speak Hungarian and send their children to Hungarian schools. Many Hungarians seek more independence from the Slovak government. Some of Hungary's leaders show sympathy toward these demands, but historically the issue has led to tension between the two nations.

Slovakia has one of the largest Roma populations in Europe. The Roma are a people who probably originally came from India. The earliest written record of them in Slovakia appeared in 1322. Also known as Romany, the Roma form about 2 percent of the population. The government has a hard time taking an accurate census of Roma, however, and some experts believe

Some demographic experts estimate that **about 380,000 Roma** were living in Slovakia in 2001.

THE STRUGGLES OF THE ROMA

Katarina and Vladimir Krusten and their six children face challenges typical for many Roma in Slovakia. Occasionally, Vladimir Krusten gets temporary jobs, but the family relies on welfare payments. They live in a one-room shack on the outskirts of a village. The shack has no running water, and Katarina Krusten says that it's difficult to stay clean. Like many Roma, the family speaks Romany at home and the children do not speak Slovak fluently. They are often behind in their education. Typically, three of the Krusten children go to a school for children with special needs, where the education is below the norm. The Krusten home has no electricity, so the children can't study after dark. It is very hard for the Roma to improve their lives under such conditions.

Two women chat in the streets of a small Slovak village near the Ukrainian border.

the number is much higher. Some Roma lead a nomadic, or wandering, lifestyle traveling from place to place. About one-third of the Roma live in wooden sheds or other poor structures on the outskirts of towns and villages. They have limited or no access to clean water, garbage pickup, electricity, or other basic public works. Isolated from the rest of Slovak society, they have faced centuries of prejudice and discrimination. As a result, they suffer high unemployment and crime rates. They also have the nation's lowest living standards. In modern Slovakia, Roma have organized political and cultural groups to work for their rights. Roma politicians have won some local and national elections.

Ruthenians make up about 1 percent of Slovakia's population. They live in Carpatho-Ruthenia, in eastern Slovakia. The region has historic ties to Ukraine. Ruthenians speak a dialect (variation) of Ukrainian and are related to the ethnic Ukrainians who live to the east. Most live in small and scattered rural villages and work in farming and forestry. Other small groups, such as Czechs, Poles, and Germans, make up the remaining 2 percent of the population.

► Language

Slovak is Slovakia's official language. It is a member of the West Slavic family of languages. This group also includes Polish and Czech. Slovak and Czech share many words in common, although certain letters and sounds are unique to each language. They may speak one of many local dialects, but Slovaks and Czechs can easily understand each other.

Slovakia's ethnic minorities speak their own languages, in addition to Slovak. Ethnic Hungarians in southern and eastern Slovakia speak Hungarian. This is a Finno-Ugric language, not related to the Slavic tongues. Hungarians want their language to have official

A woman enters a butcher shop in Bratislava.
The signs are in Slovak.

The Slovak language is written in the same Latin alphabet that English uses. But it adds four diacritical marks, or accent signs, that change the way letters sound. (This book does not use the diacritical marks.) The two most common marks are the acute, which looks like a dash above a letter, and the caron, which looks like a tiny *v*. The caron makes a sound soft, so *dž* sounds like *j* in "jam"; *š* sounds like *sh* in "shine"; and *ň* sounds like *ny*, as in "new." The acute makes a letter sound long, so *ú* sounds like the *oo* in "cool." One language expert suggests you learn the sound of *ŕ* from mimicking a dog when it *grrrrowls*.

status in Slovakia, like Slovak does. Ruthenians use a Slavic dialect related to Ukrainian. It is written in the Cyrillic alphabet. Roma speak Romany. This language is similar to languages spoken in central and northern India, where the Roma people probably originated. Most ethnic Poles and Germans speak the language of their ancestors in addition to Slovak. Students often choose to study English in school.

Education

Slovaks value education highly, and the law requires all students to attend eight years of elementary school. The government spends about 10 percent of its budget on schooling. Public and church-run schools are free. Private schools, which charge fees, have operated since the fall of Communism. Many Slovak children begin their schooling at age three, when they attend preschool. At age six, they enter elementary school. Religion is a required subject in elementary schools. Nonreligious parents can choose a class in ethics, the study of proper behavior, for their children instead.

Students may continue at a secondary school, but the government does not require secondary education. Secondary schools in Slovakia include college preparatory schools and vocational schools that offer job training.

Schoolchildren focus on their studies in an elementary school. Education is highly valued in Slovakia.

Thirty institutions offer higher education in Slovakia. They include Comenius University and the Academy of Fine Arts in Bratislava. Founded in Bratislava in 1919, Comenius University is Slovakia's oldest university. It was the first college to teach the Slovak language. Public universities are free, but they accept only a limited number of students, so competition is tough.

Slovakia's educational system produces a high literacy rate, or percentage of people aged fifteen and older who can read and write a basic sentence. In fact, the country reports that 100 percent of its young citizens are literate, with a slightly lower rate for older people.

Religion

Slovakia's constitution guarantees freedom of religion. Historically, Slovaks have been very religious. The former Communist government saw the nation's churches as rivals for citizens' loyalty. Communist leaders wanted people to adopt "scientific atheism," or to replace religious beliefs with science. Laws placed strict limits on public religious worship. Some people stopped going to religious services. Other religious groups held services underground, or in secret.

 Visit www.vgsbooks.com for links to websites with additional information about Slovakia's people, language, and religion.

The Cathedral of Saint Martin is one of Bratislava's greatest historical landmarks. Construction of this Gothic cathedral began in 1221 and took nearly two hundred years to complete.

The fall of Communism in 1989 ended forty years of religious restrictions. People restored churches and reopened some religious schools. Slovaks, who have mostly been Roman Catholic since the 800s, returned to worship services in great numbers. In the twenty-first century, many citizens report that their faith is important to them and that they attend weekly religious services.

While 69 percent of people in Slovakia are Catholic, the country is also home to several other branches of the Christian faith. Some Slovaks are Evangelical Lutheran (7 percent), Greek Catholic (4 percent), Calvinist Reformed (2 percent), and Orthodox Christian (1 percent). The Lutheran and Calvinist faiths came to Slovakia after Martin Luther's attempts to reform the Catholic Church in the sixteenth century. The Greek Catholic Church formed in the late 1500s.

WISDOM OF THE AGES

Many Slovak proverbs, or sayings, express age-old wisdom. Here are a few examples:

- Anger is the only thing to put off until tomorrow.
- A man who has enough to eat does not believe the starving man's tale.
- Don't shake the tree when the pears fall off by themselves.
- There is no wise response to a foolish remark.
- Whoever gives to me, teaches me to give.
- Even a giant oak was once an acorn.
- Love needs no laws.
- It is easier to criticize than to create.
- Fear is worse than misfortune itself.
- No work, no cake.

The Ruthenians of eastern Slovakia mostly follow this faith. It is a branch of Roman Catholicism, loyal to the Catholic pope (church leader, based in Vatican City, a state within Italy). However, it uses Orthodox rituals and texts during its services. Orthodox Christians follow the teachings of the Eastern Orthodox Church. It originated in Constantinople (modern-day Istanbul, Turkey) and later split from Roman Catholicism.

Another 3 percent of the population hold a variety of religious beliefs. A small Jewish community exists in Slovakia. However, most Slovak Jews who survived World War II chose to emigrate from Slovakia to Israel, the Jewish state in the Middle East, or to other countries. The remaining 14 percent of Slovaks practice no religion.

Lifestyles

Slovakia has become a more urban country since World War II, but many Slovaks continue to admire the traditional values of their peasant ancestors. These include hard work, a sense of humor,

Friends enjoy the afternoon on a bench in Hlavne Namestie (translated "main square"), the central square of Bratislava and a common meeting place for Slovaks.

In the cities, Slovaks typically dress in modern clothing styles. These people are wearing casual and professional business attire.

and a willingness to help one another out. Slovaks appreciate hospitality and politeness. Professional achievement is respected, and people address one another by their titles, such as "doctor" or "professor." Friends and family are less formal, but adults in formal settings call one another Pan (Mr.) or Pani (Mrs.).

Slovaks generally like to dress fashionably. They dress up for school and work. Businesspeople wear suits. Jeans and T-shirts are common in cities but less common in rural areas, where villagers tend to dress more conservatively. People in the countryside may wear their traditional costumes for festivals and special events.

Housing in cities often consists of apartment buildings constructed during the Communist era. People live in small, plain apartments, which were designed for utility rather than beauty. Slovakia has a housing shortage, so adult children often continue to live with their parents, even after they're married, until they can find a place of their own. In rural areas, single-family homes are the norm. They offer more comfort than cramped city apartments. Many city dwellers keep gardens in the country, where they grow fruits and vegetables in the summer.

Women in modern Slovakia hold equal rights under the law with men. Most women work outside the home. Traditional roles remain, however, and women are usually expected to do the housework and child care too. Grandparents often help take care of the children.

CULTURAL LIFE

Slovakia has maintained its own language and traditions in the face of larger cultural forces for centuries. The independent nation of Slovakia is not just one culture, however, but many. Hungarian, Roma, and other cultures enrich the country's music, art, and words.

Literature

Slovak-written literature dates back to the time Cyril and Methodius developed the first written script for the Slavs, in the 800s. Early works were mostly religious.

Under a thousand years of Hungarian rule, Slovaks kept alive their culture through folktales and legends. They learned historical, religious, and fanciful stories by heart and passed them on by word of mouth.

In the early 1800s, educated Slovaks wrote in Hungarian or Czech. In 1824 the Slovak clergyman Jan Kollar wrote a collection of poems, *The Daughter of Slava*, in Czech. During the 1840s, Ludovit Stur unified the many variations of Slovak into one written language. Slovaks

began to express their pride and hopes through writing. Terezia Vansova wrote realistically about village life. Her 1899 novel *The Orphan* was the first published novel by a Slovak woman. She also wrote poetry, short stories, and a cookbook, and started Slovakia's first magazine for women, *Dennica* (Daily).

Slovak literature thrived after the founding of Czechoslovakia in 1918. Stefan Zary and other Slovak poets of the 1920s often used unusual symbols and dreamlike images in their works. Zary's most famous collection of verse is *The Wandering Spider*. Martin Kukucin is known as the father of Slovak realism. Writers in this style seek to capture the experiences of common people. Kukucin described everyday life in his novels *Mother Calls* and *The House on the Slope* and in many short stories.

World War II and the rise of Communism became important subjects for postwar Slovak writers. Writers risked jail if they published work that offended the government. Novelists had to glorify the new regime and its state-run farms and factories. In *Kronika* Peter Jilemnicky praised Communist rebels and other Slovaks who fought against Slovakia's pro-German government during World War II. *The Fallow Field* was Jilemnicky's tribute to Slovak peasants.

Some Slovak writers dared to criticize Communist rule. Laco Novomesky was a poet, journalist, and politician. Though he was a Communist, Novomesky spoke out for artistic freedom. He was sentenced to prison for ten years. Dominik Tatarka denounced Communist policies in *The Demon of Consent*. Writer Ladislav Mnacko fled Czechoslovakia after the Soviet invasion of 1968 so he could express himself freely. He described the events of 1968 in *The Seventh Night*.

New possibilities arose for Slovak writers with the fall of Communism. Maria Batarova is a professor of Slovak literature as well as a writer of short stories. Her collection *Tranquility* (1996) focuses on personal relationships between men and women. The title of Milka Zimkova's collection of short stories *She Grazed Horses on Concrete* (1980) comes from a song about a woman who does impossible things. A best seller, it was made into a movie and continues to be popular in the 2000s.

Julius Balco writes for adults and children. He blends fantasy and fact in his books for children, such as his three-part series about wizards. The last volume of the series, *The Wizard's Year*, came out in 1999.

Slovak literature has not yet been widely available in English. *In Search of Homo Sapiens: Twenty-five Contemporary Slovak Short Stories* was published in English translation in 2002. It is a collection of short pieces by some of the most important Slovak writers and thinkers. Peter Pistanek's novel *Rivers of Babylon* is a darkly comic novel about criminal forces in post-Communist Slovakia. It was a best seller in Slovakia when it was published in 1991, and it was translated into English in 2007.

⊙ Art

Slovakia has a rich tradition of folk arts including wood carving and glass painting. Fabric arts include cloth weaving, fine lace making, and embroidery.

Glass holds a special place in Slovakia's art history. The first glassworks in Slovakia began operating in 1350. The land became famous for fancy hand-blown and hand-cut crystal glassware. Cheaper machine-made glass replaced handmade glass in the 1800s, but the art of fine glassblowing survives. Artisans fashion glass into useful items and fine art pieces.

After the formation of Czechoslovakia in 1918, Slovak artists chose to depict traditional Slovak scenes that reflected their unique heritage.

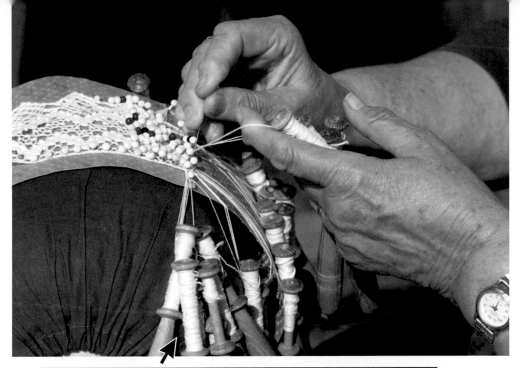

A woman in Slovakia makes lace by hand using bobbins and thread.

Milan Laluha painted rural scenes in abstract, or geometric, shapes. Red was the dominant color in his bold and richly colored paintings.

The Communist government after World War II restricted artists' freedoms. Only art in the "socialist realism" style was allowed in public. Artists were not free to express their own personal vision, and art did not thrive in this era.

Though censorship ended, modern art got little encouragement during the early years of Slovakia's independence. The country was more concerned with creating a new government and new social systems. In the twenty-first century, however, artists in Slovakia explore painting and photography as well as new computer and video arts. Oliver Lesso is a contemporary artist who mixes old and new in his glass sculptures. His strong, simple forms play with light and seem to glow inside.

GLASSBLOWING

Glassmaking companies in Slovakia produce beautiful crystal glassware in the age-old way—by melting silica, or quartz sand, at high heat and then blowing the molten glass into shape. Glassworkers work as a team. One scoops up a red-hot blob of glass out of a cauldron and places it on the end of a long, narrow tube called a blow tube. The blower blows into the tube to inflate the glass into a bubble and rotates it to spin the glass into shape. A third person takes the piece with long tongs and sets it to cool. Slovak glassblowers fear theirs is a dying art, however, as few people choose to study it anymore.

▶ Film

In 1921 Slovakia became the tenth country in the world to make feature-length films. The film was *Janosik*, about the Slovak folk hero. Under Communism, film, like all arts, had to show how happy life was in a Communist society. In the early 1960s, government control relaxed a bit. In 1962 *The Sun in a Net* marked a milestone in Slovak film. Directed by Stefan Uher, it showed society as it really was, through the troubled lives of a pair of teenagers. Slovakia's first Oscar-winning movie was *The Shop on Main Street*, in 1965. It is a grim tale of an ethnic Slovak's struggles to protect an old Jewish woman from being sent to a concentration camp during World War II.

In 1982 Stefan Uher made Milka Zimkova's story *She Grazed Horses on Concrete* into a film. Zimkova played the lead role, as a single mother raising a teenage daughter in a village. It is a humorous look at the serious issues of women's roles in Slovakia. The next year, leading Slovak filmmaker Juraj Jakubisko made *A Thousand-Year Old Bee*. It showed the way powerful people took away the results of the peasants' labor as people take honey from bees.

This is a movie still taken from *The Shop on Main Street* **(1965),** Slovakia's first Oscar-winning film.

Director Vladimir Balco filmed the best-selling novel *Rivers of Babylon* in 1998. It is about the political rise of a ruthless but stupid man. In 2008 Juraj Jakubisko released *Bathory*, his first English-language film. It presented the director's belief that the Hungarian countess Elizabeth Bathory was not a murderess as history claims. The next year saw another film about a historic figure, the ever-popular Janosik. *The True Story of Juraj Janosik and Tomas Uhorcik* was a Slovak-Polish-Czech coproduction. All three Slavic countries enjoy legends about the dashing hero and his fellow adventurer Uhorcik.

Music

Slovakia's folk music tradition is one of the richest in central Europe. In all, more than sixteen thousand Slovak folk songs have been collected and published. Hundreds of years ago, the *igric*, a singer of epic tales, entertained people in villages as well as at royal courts. Slovaks passed down folk melodies from one generation to the next. Roma, Germans, and Hungarians brought their music to Slovakia too.

Dances are also part of Slovak folk culture. They vary from region to region, and modern performers often dress in the regions' traditional costumes. Couples whirl to polkalike dances, and men perform active solo dances.

Modern composers such as the Czech Leos Janacek and the Hungarian Bela Bartok collected Slovak folk songs. They often incorporated them into their own works.

A variety of instruments accompany Slovak songs and dances. The more than one hundred kinds of flutes and pipes include the *fujara*, which is over 5 feet (1.5 m) long. Its deep tones give traditional shepherd's music a sad sound.

The fujara is a traditional Slovak instrument hand carved from the wood of deciduous trees. It was originally used by shepherds to calm the sheep as they grazed.

The *fanforka* is a reed instrument similar to a clarinet. The *gajdy* is a set of bagpipes. Small groups of musicians perform both Slovak folk and classical music on these instruments as well as violins and other stringed instruments. Ensembles may include the *cymbal* (dulcimer), a stringed instrument played with a hammer.

As with the other arts, music expanded after the Velvet Revolution of 1989. Freed from state censorship, Slovak musicians embraced western styles, from rock and pop to grunge and hip-hop. Traditional folk music and dance remains popular with young people too. Peter Dvorsky is an internationally famous Slovak opera singer.

Every summer since 1997, the city of Trencin has hosted the outdoor Pohoda Music Festival. *Pohoda* means "relax" in Slovak. Many kinds of musicians and fans, celebrating everything from classical to techno, meet and mingle at the two-day event. Besides live performances by musicians from around the world, the festival offers dance, literature, and theater workshops too.

Sports and Recreation

Soccer, called football outside the United States, is Slovakia's most popular team sport. Bratislava is the home of many professional soccer teams. Amateur teams play for many cities and towns across the country.

Ice hockey is a very popular winter sport. Bratislava and Kosice host the nation's top-rated hockey squads. Slovakia had to form a new national team after the separation of Czechoslovakia. Slovaks were thrilled when their young team won the Ice Hockey World Championship in 2002.

Slovakia's national soccer team takes on the Czech Republic in a qualifying game for the Union of European Football Associations (UEFA) championships in 2008.

Slovak athletes won three gold medals in canoeing at the 2008 Summer Olympic Games. Slovakia's Olympic athletes have also won medals in swimming, shooting, wrestling, snowboarding, and judo.

The mountains of Slovakia offer hiking, camping, and many outdoor sports. Skiers flock to resorts in the Nizke Tatry and other mountain ranges. The nation has applied to the International Olympic Committee to host the Winter Olympic Games in the future. The rocky peaks of the Mala Fatra and the High Tatras challenge mountain climbers. Mountain streams offer excellent fishing.

Cyclists can follow a 40-mile (65 km) bike trail that links Bratislava with Vienna, Austria. Swimmers and boaters enjoy the country's freshwater lakes and rivers. During the spring snowmelt, kayakers and canoeists ride the waters rushing down from the mountains of the north.

City dwellers attend movies, art exhibits, and local events. People often entertain one another with meals in their homes rather than at restaurants. For vacations, many Slovaks head to the mountains or the countryside. Gardening, picnicking, and mushroom hunting are popular family activities at summer cottages. Health spas and hot springs also attract visitors from Slovakia and elsewhere.

KOSICE'S INTERNATIONAL PEACE MARATHON

Kosice, Slovakia, hosts the oldest ongoing marathon in Europe. Except during World War II, runners have gathered in Kosice on the first Sunday of October since 1924. The 26.2-mile (42 km) course loops twice through the historic city center. In the modern world, only the marathon in Boston, Massachusetts, is older.

Holidays

In Slovakia, January 1 is not only New Year's Day but also Independence Day, celebrating the formation of the country in 1993. May 1 is Labor Day. May 8 marks the end of World War II in Europe with Victory over Fascism Day. (Nazi Germany and the pro-Nazi Slovak Republic were fascist states.) The Slovak National Uprising of 1944 is remembered on August 29, and Constitution Day is September 1.

Many Christian holidays are also official state holidays in Slovakia, with banks and other businesses closing. January 6 is Three Kings Day

Visit www.vgsbooks.com for links to websites with additional information about some of Slovakia's holidays and celebrations.

and Orthodox Christmas. Easter falls in the spring. Cyril and Methodius Day, on July 5, commemorates the arrival of the two missionaries in the Great Moravian Empire in 863. Children receive small presents on Saint Nicholas Day (December 6), but Christmas, on December 25, is the most celebrated Christian holiday. Many families gather to decorate the tree, give gifts, eat and drink, and go to church.

▶ Food

The nation's farms, lakes, and forests provide plenty of fruit, vegetables, fish, and meat. Slovaks prepare a wide variety of foods. Traditional ingredients include potatoes, wheat flour, cheese made from sheep's and cow's milk, cabbage, carrots, onions, and garlic. Pork, beef, chicken, and fish are the most common meats. Less commonly, wild game, such as roast goose, venison (deer), pheasant, and rabbit, appears on Slovak tables. Fruits include apples, pears, peaches, apricots, cherries, plums, and grapes.

Slovaks eat their main meal at midday. Bread, rice, or potatoes accompany soup, meat, and vegetables. Baked goods such as poppyseed rolls or cake are popular desserts. Breakfast and the evening meals are simpler fare of bread and rolls, with sliced ham or other meat, eggs, butter, and cheese.

The national dish is *bryndzove halusky*: small potato dumplings topped with bacon and sheep's milk cheese. Slovaks also enjoy *kapustnica*, a hearty cabbage soup.

Slovakia's cuisine shows the influence of neighboring countries. From Hungary comes goulash. This thick stew contains potatoes, green peppers, and pork and other meat. It is flavored with paprika, a sweet and hot red spice. Cooks also prepare dishes from Austria including noodles, pancakes, and rich pastries.

Bryndzove halusky, the national Slovak dish, is a very hearty meal. It is commonly served with a glass of sour milk called *zincica*.

Beer and wine are popular alcoholic beverages among adults. Dry (not sweet) white wine is a specialty from the vineyards of the Male Karpaty region. *Slivovica* is a sweet plum brandy served before meals. Diners often complete meals with a small cup of strong, thick, sweet Turkish coffee.

BRYNDZOVE HALUSKY/POTATO DUMPLINGS WITH CHEESE AND BACON

The Slovak national dish is halusky (potato dumplings) topped with *bryndza* (sheep's milk cheese) and bacon. Bryndza may be hard to find, so this recipe substitutes feta and cream cheese.

3 large potatoes	6 slices bacon
5 tablespoons flour	½ cup (4 oz.) feta cheese
1 plus 2 teaspoons salt	½ cup cream cheese
1 egg	4 tablespoons milk

1. Peel the potatoes. Grate them finely with a cheese grater or food processor. Drain on paper towels.
2. In a bowl, mix the flour with 1 teaspoon salt. Beat the egg in a different bowl. Stir the egg into the flour and salt. Blend the grated potatoes into the dough.
3. Fill a large pot halfway with water and 2 teaspoons salt. Bring to a boil.
4. Using a long-handled spoon, carefully place teaspoonfuls of the potato mixture into the boiling water.
5. Boil the halusky about 5 minutes, until the dumplings float on top of the water. Scoop them out with a strainer or slotted spoon. Drain, and keep warm in a baking dish in an oven set on low.
6. Cut bacon slices into small pieces. Cook (fry, bake, or microwave) according to package directions.
7. Prepare the cheese sauce: Place the feta, cream cheese, and milk in a pan. Stirring constantly, heat the mixture over medium heat, until the mixture is blended and begins to boil.
8. Pour the cheese sauce over the halusky. Sprinkle bacon bits on top, and serve.

Serves 4 to 6

THE ECONOMY

Since Slovakia became an independent country in 1993, economic reforms have made it one of the most successful economies of the Eastern bloc countries. The country went through many ups and downs as it moved toward a modern free enterprise system. Progress was slow at first under Prime Minister Meciar. But after he was voted out of power in 1998, the government of Prime Minister Dzurinda forged ahead with improvements.

The changes came at a high social cost at first. Closing outdated factories led to a huge loss of jobs. The economy opened up to outside investors, and some workers resented working for foreign-owned firms. But reforms in the twenty-first century helped the country compete with other European nations. The changes included privatization, or selling state-owned firms to private owners. Tax laws became simpler. Foreign investment boomed, especially in the automobile industry. The nation's earnings steadily increased. Unemployment fell from the very high 18 percent to 8 percent. All of these signs of

a healthy economy led to Slovakia being admitted to the European Union in 2004. Trade with other EU member nations helped further stabilize and strengthen Slovakia's economy.

Beginning in 2007, a financial crisis in the United States badly stressed the global economy. Slovakia's growth slowed in 2008, due to the worldwide economic downturn. A slump in car sales and factory production hit especially hard. Experts expect Slovakia's economy to recover gradually. The country's average GDP (gross domestic product, or the amount a country earns in a year) per person is $22,242, one of the highest in central and eastern Europe.

The EU requires that members have a healthy economy before they can join the eurozone and use the EU's shared currency, the euro. Slovakia met the requirements and adopted the euro in 2009. Rising costs and an increase in joblessness, however, remain big challenges for Slovakia. Corruption in business is also a concern. Mafia-like crime organizations use bribes and violence to control some Slovak businesses.

With more than fifty ski resorts in the country, skiing is a popular activity for native Slovaks and tourists alike. Here, skiers prepare to hit the slopes at a resort in the High Tatras.

Services, Tourism, and Trade

The service sector includes jobs in government and education, the financial sector, health services, tourism, retail sales, and similar industries that involve providing services instead of making goods. Slovakia's service sector earns 64 percent of Slovakia's annual GDP. This sector employs about 56 percent of workers.

Slovakia's beautiful mountain scenery, ski resorts, castles, and other historical sights attract 1.5 million tourists from other countries every year. The largest number of visitors comes from the Czech Republic, followed by Poland and Germany. Slovaks and foreigners alike relax at more than twenty spa resorts, with mineral springs. Visitors add $932 million every year to Slovakia's economy.

Slovakia's main trade items for export (sale to other countries) are vehicles, machinery, electrical equipment, metals, chemicals, and weapons. Its main customers are other EU countries, especially Germany, the Czech Republic, and France. The country records a trade deficit, meaning it imports more than it exports. It buys most of its imports from Germany, the Czech Republic, and Russia. Slovakia's fortunes are tied to its main trading partners in the eurozone area. Due to economic downturn, the economies of its neighbors are not as strong as before. The situation is expected to improve slowly.

Industry and Manufacturing

The industrial sector includes manufacturing, mining, construction, and energy businesses. Altogether, industry brings in 33 percent of

Slovakia's GDP. Industrial fields provide jobs for 38 percent of the labor force.

The main industrial centers are in Bratislava and Kosice. Factories produce metal and metal products, food and beverages, and chemicals. Glass manufacturers make glassware for homes but also fine glass parts for industrial use.

The country offers many attractions for foreign investors. The attractions include a large pool of skilled workers and fairly low taxes and labor costs. The U.S. company Whirlpool manufactures domestic appliances such as washing machines in Slovakia. Dell's headquarters for its European computer-making operations are in Bratislava.

Slovakia is one of the leading automobile makers in central Europe. Slovak factories produce about 850,000 cars a year, mostly for export. The German company Volkswagen has been making cars in Slovakia since 1991. Volkswagen is developing and building a new brand of microcars at its plant in Bratislava. These are very small, economical city cars. Besides auto assembly plants, other industries related to cars have invested in Slovakia. U.S. Steel operates in Kosice. A Spanish firm that makes car upholstery is also located in Kosice. Ten South Korean auto-parts makers help stimulate the economy.

Czechoslovakia was one of the world's leading weapons makers until 1990. Most of the weapons, artillery, and tanks factories were in Slovakia. Most of the arms were exported to Warsaw Pact countries.

Workers at Volkswagen Slovakia in Bratislava assemble Audis (a line of cars manufactured by Volkswagen). The vehicles manufactured in the Bratislava factory are primarily exported to other European countries and to the United States.

After the fall of Communism, these customers mostly stopped buying. Slovakia has converted many of its military-based factories to civilian (nonmilitary) use. The tank factory at Martin, for instance, makes earthmoving equipment and tractor engines. Slovakia is still a weapons producer, but weapons production is no longer a significant part of the economy.

Mining and Energy

Mining is a small part of the industrial sector. The main minerals are lignite (brown coal), copper, zinc, lead, iron ore, and magnesite. Uranium mines provide fuel for the nation's nuclear power plants. The construction industry relies on the land's limestone and gravel. Construction projects include expanding the nation's highway system.

Nuclear power plants provide about 56 percent of Slovakia's energy. Nuclear reactors create energy through starting and controlling nuclear chain reactions—the same reactions that lead to explosions in nuclear bombs. The energy is cheaper and causes less pollution than energy derived from burning fossil fuels. Nuclear waste is toxic and long-lasting, however. Storing the dangerous material poses a challenge. Further, a nuclear accident could cause terrible harm to people and the environment. In 2008 Slovakia shut down the entire power plant in Bohunice, due to safety concerns. The plant is 31 miles (50 km) northeast of Bratislava, near the Austrian border. Slovakia is building new, safer plants.

Power plants that burn coal and other fossil fuels generate about 30 percent of the country's electricity. Slovakia's deposits of petroleum and natural gas are not enough to meet the country's energy needs. The country must import gas and petroleum, mostly from Russia. A huge refinery in Bratislava processes the petroleum into gasoline. Dams on rivers create hydroelectric power, which meets 14 percent of the country's electricity needs.

MELTDOWN

A mint in the village of Kremnica has been making coins since the 1300s. It began making a coin called the koruna—which means "crown" in Slovak—in 1993. After Slovakia decided to adopt the euro, however, the mint began melting down korunas. The coins officially lost their value on January 17, 2009. A special machine melts down the coins, which are mostly steel with a coating of other metals. The material is then recycled. The meltdown took almost one year.

Agriculture

Agriculture was the backbone of Slovakia for centuries. Slovaks labored as peasants on Hungarian-

Wheat, grown in fields such as this one in north central Slovakia, is one of Slovakia's three main crops. Sugar beets and corn are the other two.

owned land until the formation of Czechoslovakia in 1918. At that point, Slovak farmers became the landowners. Communist rule, however, once again forced Slovak farmers to give up their lands. They pooled their land and machinery to form state-run farms. These groups had to meet government quotas and sell at prices the government set. In 1989 the new democratic government privatized the country's farmlands. Within three years, 98 percent of farms were privately owned, making Slovakia a leader in land reform among Eastern bloc countries.

The agriculture sector of the economy includes farming, fishing, and forestry. Agriculture provides 3 percent of Slovakia's GDP. It employs 6 percent of the workforce. About 51 percent of the land is used for farming. The Danubian lowland area is the most fertile part of the nation.

The main crops are sugar beets, wheat, and corn. Farmers also cultivate wine grapes, tobacco, apples, watermelons, and other fruit. The main vegetables are potatoes, cabbages, tomatoes, onions, carrots, and turnips.

Raising animals is an important farming activity. Sheep and cattle are the main livestock in the northern mountainous regions. People in villages usually raise ducks, chickens, and turkeys for their own consumption as well as to sell. Rabbits are also popular animals in the countryside. Horse breeding is widespread in Slovakia too. Horse owners often rent horses to tourists.

Commercial anglers capture carp, pike, perch, and bream. Aquaculture, or breeding fish in fishponds, is common throughout

Slovakia. Carp and trout are the most commonly bred fish. Forest products include logs for building and a small amount for fuel.

The rural economy is not as healthy as Slovaks would like. Unemployment is far higher in rural areas than in cities, and education levels in the countryside remain fairly low. Few rural people go to school beyond primary school. Farmers and their families, therefore, are not well-equipped to participate in the high-tech modern economy. Many rural people depend on government aid.

Transportation

Most Slovak families own a car. But high gas prices mean that most people rely on city buses and other public transportation rather than driving regularly. Slovakia has 27,191 miles (43,761 km) of roads, 87 percent of which are paved. Drivers can travel on 196 miles (316 km) of expressways, and more superhighways are under construction. Commercial boats can navigate 106 miles (172 km) on the Danube River.

The transport of illegal drugs across Slovakia's eastern border with Ukraine is a problem for Slovakia. The heavily forested, mountainous region is hard for Slovak police to patrol, and it's fairly close to the Austrian and Czech borders. These factors make it a favorite with smugglers. Illegal immigrants from poor areas in the east also cross this border. They are seeking better opportunities in Europe.

Slovakia's train system is efficient and inexpensive, with 2,275 miles (3,662 km) of track. Trains link Bratislava with most major towns. An express train travels from Bratislava to Vienna, Austria. Thirty-five airports offer national connections. Airports in Bratislava and Kosice handle most of the country's international flights.

Communications

The constitution guarantees freedom of the press and forbids censorship. Slovaks enjoy many newspapers and magazines. The *Slovak Spectator* is a daily English-language paper that can be read online. Many book publishers operate in the country. Slovakia's telecommunications system is modern and far-reaching. About 1.2 million landline telephones and 6 million cell phones are in use.

Almost every home in Slovakia has a television and radio. Satellite and cable TV is popular, and many viewers watch channels from the

Czech Republic and Hungary. Eighty television stations and dozens of radio stations broadcast throughout the country. Computers are also widespread, with half the population using the Internet.

▶ The Future

Slovakia is a young country, with a young tradition of democratic politics and economics. Its progress has been impressive. Many Slovaks believe that it is a wise policy to work hard and to invest money in education and technology. In less than a dozen years after independence in 1993, Slovakia turned around an inefficient, out-of-date economy. A government committed to reform helped prepare the country for entrance into the European Union in 2004. The adoption of the euro in 2009 signaled how far the new country has come.

Corruption and unemployment saddle the economy, however, and unequal opportunities for the Roma challenge society. A global economic recession, beginning in 2008, severely slowed Slovakia's growth. The nation's—and the world's—road to full recovery may be long. But the nation has a firm foundation. Slovakia waited hundreds of years for independence, and many Slovaks believe patience pays off.

Visit www.vgsbooks.com for links to websites with additional information about current events in Slovakia.

CA. 23,000 B.C.   A Stone Age artist in Slovakia carves a little sculpture of a woman out of a mammoth tusk. In modern times, it is called the Moravian Venus.

CA. 6000 B.C.   Farming groups begin to settle permanently in the Danubian lowland.

CA. 500 B.C.   People called Celts spread from the west into Slovakia. They make the area's first metal coins.

A.D. 172   The Roman emperor Marcus Aurelius leads his troops against a Germanic tribe in Slovakia. While in Slovakia, the emperor writes part of his famous book *Meditations*.

CA. 500   Slavs arrive in Slovakia. They are the ancestors of modern Slovaks, Czechs, Poles, and others.

833   Slavic prince Mojmir founds a new state in western Slovakia and Moravia called the Great Moravian Empire.

906   The Magyars, ancestors of modern Hungarians, defeat the Great Moravian Empire and establish the Kingdom of Hungary. Hungarian landowners hold most of the power in the kingdom, while most Slovaks labor as serfs.

1241   People from eastern Asia called Mongols invade Slovakia, inspiring Hungarian landowners to begin to build castles for defense.

1526   Ottoman Turks conquer Buda, the Hungarian capital, and kill the Hungarian king in battle. The Austrian king, Ferdinand, a member of the powerful Habsburg dynasty, becomes the king of Hungarian lands.

1610   Hungarian countess Elizabeth Bathory is arrested in Slovakia for her supposed murder of dozens of young women.

1618   A rebellion against Catholic Habsburg rule in Prague (capital of the present-day Czech Republic) touches off the Thirty Years' War (1618-1648) between Europe's Catholic and Protestant states.

1740   Empress Maria Theresa inherits the throne of the Habsburg Empire. Her rule will improve the lives of Slovaks.

1848   Slovak nationalists hold a Slavic Congress in Prague to demand self-rule.

1867   Austria-Hungary, also called the Austro-Hungarian Empire, forms. Hungarian leaders make Hungarian the official language in Slovakia.

1918   Slovak leader Milan Stefanik and members of the Czechoslovak National Council establish the new nation of Czechoslovakia.

1921   Slovakia becomes the tenth country in the world to make feature-length films.

1924   The city of Kosice holds its first International Peace Marathon.

1939   Josef Tiso declares Slovakia's independence from Czechoslovakia, but the country takes orders from Germany during World War II.

1944   Rebels stage the Slovak National Uprising against Slovakia's pro-German government, but German troops defeat them.

1948   Czech Communists, with Soviet support, take over the government of reunited Czechoslovakia.

1965   *The Shop on Main Street* becomes Slovakia's first Oscar-winning movie.

1968   A Soviet-led invasion of Prague on August 20 ends the period of reform known as Prague Spring.

1989   The Velvet Revolution leads to the peaceful downfall of Communist rule in Czechoslovakia. Other Eastern bloc nations also overturn Communist rule.

1993   On January 1, Slovakia becomes a free and independent country.

2000   Slovak racists brutally murder a fifty-year-old Roma woman named Anastazia Balazova.

2002   Slovakia's national team wins the Ice Hockey World Championship.

2004   Slovakia officially joins the European Union and NATO. Ivan Gasparovic becomes president.

2005   The United Nations Educational, Scientific, and Cultural Organization (UNESCO) names the fujara (Slovak shepherds' pipe) and its music Masterpieces of the Oral and Intangible Heritage of Humanity.

2008   A worldwide economic downturn begins to slow Slovakia's economy severely. The nuclear power plant in Bohunice is shut down due to safety concerns.

2009   President Gasparovic wins reelection. Slovakia adopts the euro, the common currency of the EU. Slovakia marks the fortieth anniversary of the Velvet Revolution.

2010   The city council of Ostrovany, in eastern Slovakia, pays to build a 495-foot-long (150 m) wall to cut off a Roma settlement from the rest of the city.

COUNTRY NAME Slovakia

AREA 18,932 square miles (49,033 sq. km)

MAIN LANDFORMS Highland region; Lowland region; Danubian lowland; Slovensky Kras plateau; Carpathian mountain ranges: High Tatras, Nizke Tatry (Low Tatras), Mala Fatra (Lesser Fatra), Male Karpaty, Slovak Ore, Vel'ka Fatra (Greater Fatra); Rye Island

HIGHEST POINT Gerlach Peak 8,707 feet (2,857 m)

LOWEST POINT Bodrok River, 308 feet (94 m) above sea level

MAJOR RIVERS Danube, Hornad, Hron, Morava, Nitra, Vah

ANIMALS alpine marmots, bats, brown bears, chamois, eagles, foxes, great bustards, otters, owls, pike, trout, voles, weasels, wolves

CAPITAL CITY Bratislava

OTHER MAJOR CITIES Banska Bystrica, Kosice, Nitra, Presov

OFFICIAL LANGUAGE Slovak

MONETARY UNITY Euro. 100 cents = 1 euro.

SLOVAKIAN CURRENCY

Slovakia adopted the euro, the shared currency of the European Union, in 2009. The government then took the Slovak koruna, in use since 1993, out of circulation. Slovakia became the sixteenth EU member to join the eurozone, or the group of EU nations that use the euro. Euro coins come in denominations of 1, 2, 5, 10, 20, and 50 cents. There are also

1 and 2 euro coins. Paper bills, or banknotes, come in amounts of 5, 10, 20, 50, 100, 200, and 500 euros. The symbol of the euro is €. One side of the coins looks the same in every country. Each country chooses a design for the other side of the coins. Both sides of the banknotes are the same for every country.

Slovakia's flag consists of three horizontal stripes of equal width. Slovakia's coat of arms sits slightly to the left in the flag's center. From the top down, the stripes are white, blue, and red. These colors are also common on the flags of other nations with Slavic roots, such as Slovenia and Russia. The coat of arms is a red shield. Inside the shield, a white double cross sits atop three blue hills.

In 1844 Janko Matuska wrote the words of Slovakia's national anthem and set them to an old folk tune. Writing during the rise of Slovak national pride, Matuska used the image of lightning striking the Tatra Mountains to urge Slovaks to wake up. The first verse of the Slovak song became part of the national anthem of Czechoslovakia, when that nation formed in 1918. When Slovakia became independent in 1993, the new nation used both verses of Matuska's original song. Here is the song with lyrics translated into English.

Lightning over the Tatras
Lighting flashes over the Tatras, the thunder pounds wildly.
Lighting flashes over the Tatras, the thunder pounds wildly.
Let us pause, brothers, they will surely disappear, the Slovaks will revive,
Let us pause, brothers, they will surely disappear, the Slovaks will revive.

This Slovakia of ours has been fast asleep until now,
This Slovakia of ours has been fast asleep until now.
But the thunder and lighting are encouraging it to come alive,
But the thunder and lighting are encouraging it to come alive.

 For a link to a site where you can listen to Slovakia's national anthem, visit www.vgsbooks.com.

MIKULAS DZURINDA (b. 1955) was born in Spissky Stvrtok in eastern Slovakia. After the fall of Communist rule, he became the minister of transportation. Five years after Slovakia's independence, in 1998 he became prime minister of Slovakia. His second term ended in 2006. As prime minister, he guided Slovakia toward reforms that prepared it to join the European Union. Dzurinda founded and is the chair of the political party the Slovak Democratic and Christian Union. Married with two children, he is also an active athlete. He has run the International Peace Marathon in Kosice more than a dozen times.

JOSEF GABCIK (1912–1942) was a Slovak soldier who became a national hero for his role in the Slovak resistance to Nazi Germany during World War II. Gabcik was born in Palosnya in Austria-Hungary (modern Poluvsie, Slovakia). In 1942 he and Jan Kubis assassinated Reinhard Heydrich, an important Nazi official. After an extensive search, German forces found Gabcik and Kubis's hiding place. Gabcik committed suicide before the Nazis could reach him, and Kubis was killed in the fighting. Slovakia honored Gabcik by naming a village and a special regiment of the Slovak Army after him.

DANIELA HANTUCHOVA (b. 1983) is a professional Slovak tennis player. Born in Poprad, she went pro in 1999, when she was sixteen. She qualified for college but decided to pursue tennis instead. Hantuchova has won two Women's Tennis Association (WTA) singles tournaments, in 2002 and in 2007. In 2009 at the famous Wimbledon tennis tournament in England, she won three rounds before losing the fourth to tennis star Serena Williams. The WTA ranks Hantuchova number 26 out of hundreds of players.

FRANTISEK HOSSA (b. 1954) is a retired ice hockey player who coaches the Slovak men's national ice hockey team. Born in Smizany, Hossa also coached his sons Marian and Marcel when they were growing up. Both became hockey players, and Hossa coached them for the Slovak team during the 2006 Winter Olympics. Marian Hossa plays for the Chicago Blackhawks, and Marcel Hossa plays for a Latvian team.

JURAJ JAKUBISKO (b. 1938) Born in Kojsov, Slovakia, Jakubisko is an internationally known Slovak film director. He taught photography in Bratislava before he moved to Prague to study film in 1960. After the Soviet invasion of Prague in 1968, Jakubisko's work was heavily censored, and he made few films. The movie *A Thousand-Year-Old Bee* (1983) shows the hardships and injustice in the lives of three generations of peasants. In 1993 Jakubisko and his wife, actress and producer Deana Jakubiskova-Horvathova, set up the Jakubisko Film Company in Prague. In 2002 the Slovakian government awarded the director the Pribina Cross for his important work in Slovak film. Jakubisko released his first English-language film, *Bathory*, in 2008. It retells the

Famous People

story of Hungarian countess Bathory in Slovakia, accused of being a serial killer. He filmed the movie in castles throughout Slovakia and the Czech Republic.

JURAJ JANOSIK (1688–1713) was a Slovak robber who attacked travelers on the roads. He was probably born in present-day Tyerhova, Slovakia, then part of the Kingdom of Hungary. He was hung for his crimes but became a popular hero in the Slavic countries of Slovakia, Poland, and Czechoslovakia. Legend made him into a Robin Hood-like character who stole from the rich and gave to the poor and offered justice to oppressed people. He has been the subject of songs, stories, and art for hundreds of years. In modern times, a TV series and several films have told the adventures of Janosik.

ADRIANA KAREMBEU (b. 1971) is an international fashion supermodel. Born in Brezno, she studied medicine but gave it up to pursue her career as a model. Karembeu has acted in small roles in films and television. In 2008 she appeared in the French film *Asterix at the Olympic Games*, one of a series of comedy-adventure movies about the comic-book hero Asterix.

IVETA RADICOVA (b. 1956) was born in Bratislava, where she studied sociology at Comenius University. She became a politician and served as the Slovak minister of labor from 2005 to 2006. She is a member of the Slovak Democratic and Christian Union–Democratic Party, which is a coalition with former prime minister Dzurinda's party. Radicova ran for president of Slovakia against President Gasparovic in 2009. She came in second, with 44 percent of the votes.

PETER STASTNY (b. 1956) is a retired Slovak ice hockey player. He moved to Canada to play professionally. He played in the National Hockey League from 1980 to 1995. In 1998 he was entered in the Hockey Hall of Fame. After he retired, Slovaks elected him to represent them as a member of the European Parliament, the legislature for the European Union. He was reelected in 2009.

MILKA ZIMKOVA (b. 1951) was born in Okruzna. She is a Slovak writer and actor. Her collection of short stories *She Grazed Horses on Concrete* (1980) was a best seller and is still in print in Slovakia. Zimkova played the lead role in the 1982 movie of the same name. The movie was based on one of the stories about the life of a single mother and her daughter growing up in a Slovak village. Its U.S. title is *She Kept Crying for the Moon*. The actor performs in her own Single Actor Theatre in Slovakia and abroad.

BRATISLAVA A walking tour is one of the best ways to see some highlights of Slovakia's capital city. Start at the nineteenth-century Grassalkovich Palace and stroll through the major shopping district. Pass the monument to the Slovak National Uprising, then down the lane beside the Old Town Hall from the 1500s, where you can tour an old torture chamber. Wander through the city's central market, then head to the famous Cathedral of Saint Martin. Across from the church, climb the royal stairway to Bratislava Castle. From its ramparts, you can see the Danube River. Several museums are close by, including the excellent Museum of Jewish Culture. Musicians perform live at the Museum of Folk Music.

ICE CAVES Slovakia has two ice caves, where a year-round temperature of 30°F (−1°C) with 98 percent humidity create perfect conditions for ice to settle and form. The Dobsina ice cave is a UNESCO World Heritage Site. The Demonova ice cave is part of the biggest interconnected cave system in Slovakia. It connects to the Demanova Cave of Freedom, with its bizarre waterfalls, dramatic rock forms, and a winding mile (2 km) of underground passages.

KOSICE The yearly International Peace Marathon, on the first Sunday of October, is a lively time to visit Kosice in eastern Slovakia. The city's well-preserved city center includes the nineteenth-century Forgach Palace and the beautiful Saint Elizabeth's Cathedral, a church built between 1378 and 1508. The Eastern-Slovakia Museum displays the Gold Treasure of Kosice, a hoard of gold coins and other gold items.

MALA FATRA and **VEL'KA FATRA** These beautiful, forested mountain ranges in central Slovakia are easy to explore. In warm weather, bike through scenic valleys, walk on paths through the woods, or hike more challenging mountain trails. In winter, ski the areas' many slopes. Visitors can camp in the Mala (Lesser) Fatra National Park; stay in one of the ski resorts or mountain chalets, open year-round; or stay in one of the towns nestled in the mountain landscape. Historic castles, museums, and churches abound in the region. The tiny, picturesque village of Vlkolinec, from the 1300s, is tucked among the Vel'ka Fatra range. Vlkolinec's wooden buildings offer a unique glimpse into Slovakia's past, and the village is a UNESCO World Heritage Site.

THE SLOVAK NATIONAL MUSEUM This is a network of eighteen specialized museums throughout Slovakia. They include the Museum of Puppet Cultures and Toys in a castle in Modry Kamen. Displays in the Museum of Roma Culture in Martin show the arts and history of the Roma. The branch in the Bratislava Castle houses weapons, furniture, and folk crafts. A special exhibit presents the Slovak resistance heroes of World War II.

Austria-Hungary: also called the Austro-Hungarian Empire. The Habsburg dynasty ruled this central European state, which existed from 1867 to 1918. Slovakia was under the rule of the Kingdom of Hungary in this state.

Charter 77: the human rights document Slovak and Czech reformers signed in 1977

Cold War: the period between the end of World War II and the fall of the Soviet Union in 1991 when rivalry and tensions between the world's two superpowers, the United States and the Soviet Union, ran dangerously high

Communism: a political and economic theory that believes in common ownership of all property. Its goal is to create equality, but its practice in the Eastern bloc led to the loss of human rights and economic decline.

Eastern bloc: the Communist nations of central and Eastern Europe, including Czechoslovakia. The Eastern bloc countries were part of the Warsaw Pact's military alliance and were under Soviet control during the Cold War.

European Union (EU): an organization of nations in Europe whose purpose is to further economic cooperation, democracy, rule of law, and peace among its members

gross domestic product (GDP): the value of the goods and services produced by a country over a period of time, usually one year

nationalist: a person or group who feels supreme loyalty toward their nation and strongly promotes a national culture and national interests, including independence

NATO: the North Atlantic Treaty Organization, an alliance of the United States and the non-Communist countries of Western Europe formed after World War II for mutual defense

Prague Spring: the hopeful period in 1968 that was the result of a reform movement in Czechoslovakia. The Soviet-led invasion of Prague, Czechoslovakia, in 1968 ended the reforms.

serfs: peasants who were required to serve their lord and were not free to leave the land they worked and lived on. Serfdom was a form of slavery.

Socialism: a variety of social systems in which the government controls and manages some part of the production and distribution of goods. Socialism is a less extreme form of Communism.

Velvet Revolution: the fairly peaceful pro-democracy movement that led to the fall of Communist rule in Czechoslovakia in 1989. The relatively smooth nature of the drastic change in government led to this name.

Warsaw Pact: a political and military alliance the Soviet Union founded in 1955 in response to NATO. Czechoslovakia was an early member. The Soviet Union used the pact to control members in central and Eastern Europe. The pact dissolved in 1991, when the Soviet Union ceased to exist.

Selected Bibliography

Amnesty International. "Slovakia: Roma Children and the Right to Education." November 15, 2007.
http://www.amnestyusa.org/document.php?lang=e&id=ENGEUR720052007 (June 1, 2009).
This fact sheet provides an overview of the status of the Roma in Slovakia, with a special focus on the plight of children who do not receive equal opportunities in education.

Central Intelligence Agency. "The World Factbook: Slovakia." *The World Factbook.* **2010.**
https://www.cia.gov/library/publications/the-world-factbook/geos/lo.html (April 20, 2010).
The U.S. Central Intelligence Agency (CIA) provides this general profile of Slovakia. The profile includes brief summaries of the nation's geography, people, government, economy, communications, transportation, and military.

Czech Television. "Juraj Jakubisko." 2008.
http://www.ceskatelevize.cz/specialy/bathory/en/crew/juraj-jakubisko/ (May 13, 2009).
This online biography outlines the career of Slovak film director Juraj Jakubisko. Links lead to information about Jakubisko's 2008 film *Bathory.*

Economist. **"Country Briefings: Slovakia." 2010.**
http://www.economist.com/countries/Slovakia (April 20, 2010).
The online version of the weekly newspaper the *Economist* provides a fact sheet of economic and political data. The site also links to recent articles on Slovakia's economy and politics.

European Central Bank. *Contemporary Art from Slovakia.* **2006.**
http://www.ecb.int/events/pdf/art/Slovakia.pdf (April 23, 2010).
This is a catalog of a 2006 show of contemporary Slovak artists, part of a series of art exhibitions from member states of the European Union. Short biographies of the artists accompany pictures of their art.

Farkas, Zdenek. "The Moravian Venus." *Slovak Spectator.* **November 1, 2004.**
http://www.spectator.sk/articles/view/17719 (May 18, 2009).
This article about the Stone Age "Moravian Venus" statue is from the Slovak National Museum's regular column in the English-language *Slovak Spectator.*

Federal Research Division, Library of Congress. *A Country Study: Czechoslovakia (Former).* **Washington, DC: Federal Research Division, Library of Congress, 1989. Available online at http:// lcweb2.loc.gov/frd/cs/cstoc.html.**
This thorough study of the nation that spilt into the Czech Republic and Slovakia in 1993 includes extensive coverage of their shared history. The book also covers Slovakia's society, culture, economy, government, and politics.

Kosice Peace Marathon. **2010.**
http://www.kosicemarathon.com/en/ (April 20, 2010).
The historic city of Kosice hosts Europe's oldest continuous marathon race on the first Sunday of October. This official race site provides the history of the race, photographs, information about visiting Kosice, and registration forms to enter the race.

"PRB 2008 World Population Data Sheet." *Population Reference Bureau (PRB).* **2010.**
http://www.prb.org (April 20, 2010).
This annual statistics sheet provides a wealth of population, demographic, and health statistics for Slovakia and almost all countries in the world.

Slovak Proverbs and Sayings. N.d.
http://www.shsnepa.org/Slovak%20Proverbs%20&%20Sayings.htm. (May 14, 2009).
This list of traditional sayings includes the original Slovak phrase and a pronunciation guide.

The Statesman's Yearbook: The Politics, Cultures, and Economics of the World, 2009. New York: St. Martin's Press, 2009.
This annual publication provides concise information on Slovakia's history, climate, government, economy, and culture, including relevant statistics.

UNDP. "Human Development Report 2007/2008: Slovakia." 2008.
http://hdrstats.undp.org/countries/country_fact_sheets/cty_fs_SVK.html (June 15, 2009).
The UNDP (United Nations Development Project) provides a wide range of data reflecting countries' development. This fact sheet on Slovakia covers carbon dioxide levels as well as health, education, and other indicators of a country's human development.

U.S. Department of State, Bureau of European and Eurasian Affairs. "Background Note: Slovkia." *U.S. Department of State.* **2010.**
http://www.state.gov/r/pa/ei/bgn/3430.htm (April 20, 2010).
This website provides a general profile of Slovakia, produced by the U.S. Department of State. The profile includes brief summaries of the nation's geography, people, government and politics, and economy.

Votruba, Martin. "Historical and National Background of Slovak Filmmaking." *KinoKultura.* **January 8, 2006.**
http://www.kinokultura.com/specials/3/votruba.shtml#cz1918 (June 14, 2009).
Votruba is a professor of Slovak studies at the University of Pittsburgh in Pennsylvania. He wrote this article about this history of Slovak film for the online journal *KinoKultura*. It devoted an issue to Slovak cinema, which you can see here: http://www.kinokultura.com/specials/3/slovak.shtml.

BBC News
http://news.bbc.co.uk/
This website is a good international news source. It contains regularly updated political and cultural news. The BBC's country profile of Slovakia is found at http://news.bbc.co.uk/2/hi/europe/country_profiles/1108491.stm.

Brendel, Toni. *Slovak American Touches: Family Recipes, History, Folk Arts*. Iowa City: Penfield Books, 2008.
Along with traditional Slovak recipes, this illustrated book discusses folk art, decorative eggs and other folk arts, folk dancers, musicians, and holiday traditions.

Duberstein, John. *A Velvet Revolution: Vaclav Havel and the Fall of Communism*. Greensboro, NC: Morgan Reynolds, 2006.
This is a biography of Vaclav Havel, the pro-democracy writer who became the first president of Czechoslovakia in 1989, after the Velvet Revolution brought down Communist rule. The book includes how Havel oversaw the Velvet Divorce that led to Slovakia's independence.

Europa: The European Union at a Glance
http://europa.eu/abc/index_en.htm
The website of the European Union gives brief explanations of what this group is, what its aims and achievements are, and how it works. Basic statistics, answers to FAQs (frequently asked questions), travel tips, and more are also available. A brief entry on Slovakia is found here: http://europa.eu/abc/european_countries/eu_members/slovakia/index_en.htm

Goldstein, Margaret J. *World War II: Europe*. Minneapolis: Twenty-First Century Books, 2004.
This book gives a detailed overview of the events of World War II in Europe.

Gottfried, Ted. *Slovakia*. New York: Marshall Cavendish, 2005.
This book for younger readers offers an introduction to the geography, history, government, economy, people, and culture of Slovakia. It is part of the Cultures of the World series.

Hudki, Pavol, Heather Trebaticka, and Lucy Bednar, eds. *In Search of Homo Sapiens: Twenty-Five Contemporary Slovak Short Stories*. Mundelein, IL: Bolchazy-Carducci, 2002.
A collection of short stories by the leading Slovak writers and thinkers of recent times. A short biography and a few words by each author accompanies every entry. Excerpts from this book can be seen at http://books.google.com/books?id=oJPSb8sLve0C&source=gbs_navlinks_s.

Hurd, Margaret. *The Foreigner's Guide to Living in Slovakia*. San Diego: Modra, 2007.
This book gives tips travelers need to know about the Slovak people and how to adjust to the country. It features descriptions of Slovak food, public transportation, social and business customs, and more. The author also writes a blog, *The Foreigner's Guide to Living in Slovakia*, at http://www.fgslovakia.com/blog. She discusses food, culture, architecture, language, and other curiosities she notices as a foreigner living in Slovakia.

Further Reading and Websites

Kinkade, Sheila. *Children of Slovakia.* **Minneapolis: Lerner Publications Company, 2001.**
Part of the World's Children series, this book is illustrated with color photographs. It follows the daily lives of several children in Slovakia.

Kirschbaum, Stanislav J. *A History of Slovakia: The Struggle for Survival.* **New York: Palgrave Macmillan, 2005.**
A modern and scholarly but clearly written history of Slovakia.

Sherman, Josepha. *The Cold War.* **Minneapolis: Twenty-First Century Books, 2004.**
This entry in the Chronicle of America's Wars series discusses the events leading up to and defining the Cold War.

Slovak Spectator
http://www.spectator.sk/
Slovakia's only English-language newspaper covers politics, culture, sports, and more. The website is updated daily.

Slovak Studies Program, University of Pittsburgh
http://www.pitt.edu/~votruba/sstopics/sstopics.html
The University of Pittsburgh is the only university in the United States where students can study Slovak language and culture and earn a minor in Slovak studies. (Many Slovaks historically emigrated from Slovakia to Pittsburgh, Pennsylvania.) This site has many links to helpful and interesting sites about many aspects of Slovak history, culture, and more.

Taus-Bolstad, Stacy. *Czech Republic in Pictures.* **Minneapolis: Twenty-First Century Books, 2003.**
This book covers the land, history, people, culture, and economy of the Czech Republic. The country and Slovakia were both part of the Kingdom of Hungary and together formed the nation of Czechoslovakia from 1918 to 1993.

UNESCO World Heritage: "Slovakia"
http://whc.unesco.org/en/statesparties/sk/
UNESCO is a United Nations agency that lists World Heritage Sites. To be listed, "sites must be of outstanding universal value," either cultural or natural. This website describes Slovakia's seven World Heritage Sites, including the beech forests of the Carpathians. It also describes many more sites being considered for addition to the list.

vgsbooks.com
http://www.vgsbooks.com
Visit vgsbooks.com, the home page of the Visual Geography Series®, which is updated regularly. You can get linked to all sorts of useful online information, including geographical, historical demographic, cultural, and economic websites. The vgsbooks.com site is a great resource for late-breaking news and statistics about Slovakia and other nations.

Wilson, Neil, and Richard Nebesky. *Czech & Slovak Republics.* **Melbourne, Australia: Lonely Planet, 2001.**
This colorfully illustrated travel guide includes sections on history and culture of Slovakia, as well as maps, glossaries, and other useful information. Special coverage includes historic castles and folk culture.

Index

AIDS, 39–40
airplane crash, 36
alphabets, 23, 43
animals, 9, 14–15, 63–64; bees, 15, 52; chamois, 14; ice age, 14
arts and crafts, 33, 50–51; glass, 50, 51
Austria, 8, 25, 38
Austria-Hungary, 27–28

Bathory, Elizabeth, 25, 53, 71
Blood Countess, 25, 53, 71
Bohemia and Moravia, 22, 28, 34
Bratislava Castle, 72, 80

carbon dioxide (CO_2), 16
Carpathian Mountains, 8–9, 11, 72, 80
cars, 58, 59, 61, 64
castles, 17, 23, 71
Cathedral of Saint Martin, 18, 45
caves, 11, 72
Celts, 20–21
censorship, 5, 32, 33, 34, 49–50, 51, 54, 70
center of Europe, 7
Charter 77, 33
cities and villages, 7, 17–19, 72; Bratislava, 12, 15, 17–18, 45, 61, 62, 72, 80; Kosice, 15, 18–19, 23, 72
clothing, 47, 80
Cold War, 31
communications, 64–65
Communism, 5, 7, 18, 28, 30–34, 49–50, 51, 63
corruption and crime, 34–35, 59, 64, 65
Cyril and Methodius, 23
Czechoslovakia, 28, 29, 30–34, 61; founding of, 5, 28; split of, 7, 34
Czech Republic, 7, 8, 34, 38

Danube River, 12, 21, 23, 64, 80
Danubian lowland, 12, 14, 20, 63, 66, 68
democracy, 30, 32, 34, 35
discrimination, 34, 35, 65
Dubcek, Alexander, 32–33
Dzurinda, Mikulas, 7, 35, 58, 70

Eastern bloc, 31, 33, 63
economy, 36–37; agriculture, 19, 62–64; Communist, 31–32; global

downturn, 59, 65; industry and manufacturing, 16, 18, 19, 59, 60–62; mining, 15, 16, 62; services, 60; shipbuilding, 13; trade, 60
education, 19, 26, 41, 43–44, 65
energy and electricity, 16, 62
environmental issues, 16–17, 18, 40
ethnic groups, 7, 11, 17, 20–21, 22, 23, 34, 35, 40–42; Hungarians, 34, 41, 42–43; languages of, 42–43; Roma, 7, 30, 34, 35, 41–42, 43, 65; Slavs, 22, 40, 52
euro, 7, 11, 36, 59
European Union (EU), 7, 35–37, 59, 71

farms and farming, 4, 12, 16, 56, 62–64; historic, 20, 23, 25–26, 31, 52, 62–63
Fico, Robert, 36
films, 52–53, 70–71
floods, 11
food, 47, 56–57, 63; recipe, 57
forests, 9, 13, 14, 16, 56

Gabcik, Josef, 70
Gasparovic, Ivan, 7, 36
glacial relicts, 14
glaciers, 9, 13
glasnost, 33
glassmaking, 51, 61
global warming, 16
Gorbachev, Mikhail, 33
gross domestic product (GDP), 59, 60–61, 63

Habsburg rule, 24–28
Hantuchova, Daniela, 70
Havel, Vaclav, 33
health, 16, 39–40
history, 4–5, 7, 17, 20–37, 70; ancient, 20–21; Austria-Hungary, 27–28; Communist era, 5, 7, 18, 28, 30–34, 49–50, 51, 63; Great Moravian Empire, 4, 22–23; Hungarian rule, 4, 23–28; independence, 34–35; nationalism, 26–28, 34; pro-Nazi rule, 19, 29–30, 55, 70; Romans, 21–22
Hitler, Adolf, 29, 30
holidays, 55
Hossa, Frantisek, 19, 70
housing, 19, 20, 41, 47

human rights, 7, 34, 35, 36
Hungary, 8, 35, 38, 56; rules
  Slovakia, 4, 23–28
Hus, Jan, 24

ice hockey, 19, 54, 70
independence, 34–35
Internet use, 65

Jakubisko, Juraj, 52, 53, 70–71
Janosik, Juraj, 52, 53, 71

Karembeu, Adriana, 71
Krivan Mountain, 11

languages, 5, 23, 26, 34, 41, 42–43,
  50; Hungarian, 5, 27, 34, 41;
  Romany, 41; Slovak, 23, 43, 49
life expectancy, 40
lifestyles, 17–19, 38, 46–47, 55, 64
literacy, 44
literature, 19, 23, 33, 48–50, 71

marathon race, 55, 70, 72
Marcus Aurelius, 22
Maria Theresa (empress), 26
Meciar, Vladimir, 7, 34–35, 58
Mojmir, Prince, 22
money, 7, 11, 59, 62
mountains, 8–9, 11, 13, 15, 55, 72;
  highest peak, 9; on money, 11
music and dance, 33, 53–54, 80;
  fujara pipe, 53

nationalism, 26–28, 34
national parks, 11, 17, 19
NATO, 31, 35, 36
natural resources, 15–16
newspapers and mass media, 27, 64
nuclear power, 16, 17, 62

Ottoman Empire, 19, 24, 25

pollution, 16–17, 18, 40
Prague Spring, 32
Pribina, Prince, 19, 22
proverbs, 45

Radicova, Iveta, 37, 71
rainfall, 15

Rain Miracle, 22
religion, 43, 44–46; ancient, 27;
  Christianity, 19, 22–23, 24, 25,
  45–46, 55–56; under Communism,
  44–45; Judaism, 30, 46
rivers and lakes, 9, 12–13, 64
roads, 64
Roma (Gypsies), 7, 30, 34, 35, 43, 65;
  language of, 41–42

sanitation, 41, 42
serfs, 23, 26
Slovakia: anthem, 69; boundaries, size,
  and location, 8, 12; climate, 15, 16;
  currency, 7, 36, 68; flag, 69; flora
  and fauna, 9, 13–15; government,
  37; maps, 6, 10; population, 7, 17,
  38–39; topography, 4, 8–13
Slovak National Uprising, 19, 30, 50,
  55, 70
Soviet Union, 30, 31, 32, 33, 34
sports and recreation, 54–55, 60, 70,
  71
Stastny, Peter, 71
Stefanik, Milan, 28
Stur, Ludovit, 26, 48–49

television, 64–65
Thirty Years' War, 24–25
Tiso, Josef, 29, 30
tourism, 11, 19, 60, 72, 80
transportation, 12, 36, 55, 64
trees, 13, 14

Ukraine, 8, 42
United States, 27, 31, 61

Velvet Revolution, 7, 33–34
Vienna, Austria, 25

wars, 22, 23, 31, 36; Thirty Years',
  24–25; World War I, 5, 28; World
  War II, 19, 29–30
Warsaw Pact, 31, 33, 36, 61
weapons trade, 61–62
West, the, 31
women, 27, 36, 37, 47, 49, 50, 52,
  70, 71

Zimkova, Milka, 50, 52, 71

Captions for photos appearing on cover and chapter openers:

Cover: The ruins of ancient Spis Castle, built in the twelfth century, sit in eastern Slovakia. Spis Castle is a tourist destination and has also been the location for the filming of a number of Hollywood movies, including *Dragonheart* (1996). Spis Castle is on UNESCO's list of World Heritage Sites.

pp. 4–5 Bratislava, the capital city and cultural hub of Slovakia, lies on the banks of the Danube River.

pp. 8–9 Part of the Carpathian Mountains, the Western Tatras are Slovakia's second-largest mountain range. With challenging trails and peaks reaching as high as 7,375 feet (2,248 m), the rugged slopes are popular tourist destinations for ambitious hikers and skiers.

pp. 38–39 Slovakians meet for an evening on the town at sidewalk cafés in the historic section of Bratislava.

pp. 48–49 Traditional Slovak dancers perform at a folk festival north of Poprad, Slovakia. Folklore festivals are held every summer throughout the country to celebrate the nation's rich cultural heritage.

pp. 58–59 Novy Most, or "new bridge" in English, stretches across the Danube River in Bratislava. Visitors to the UFO restaurant *(on the far end of the bridge)*, named for its flying-saucer shape, are rewarded with a stunning view of the city.

Photo Acknowledgments

The images in this book are used with the permission of: © Jozef Sedmak/ Alamy, pp. 4–5, 51; © XNR Productions, pp. 6, 10; © Jan Wlodarczyk/Alamy, pp. 8–9; © JTB Photo Communications, Inc./Alamy, pp. 11, 53; © Juraj Bartos/ Art Directors & TRIP, pp. 12, 40; © Paul Glendell/Alamy, p. 13; © Blickwinkel/ Alamy, p. 14; © Richard Nebesky/Robert Harding Picture Library Ltd/Alamy, p. 16; © Eric Nathan/Alamy, p. 17; © Martin Barlow/Art Directors & TRIP, p. 18; The Art Archive/Gianni Dagli Orti, p. 23; The Granger Collection, New York, pp. 24, 26 (left); © Mary Evans Picture Library/Alamy, p. 25; © Adam Slinger/ Alamy, p. 26 (right); © Profimedia International s.r.o./Alamy, p. 28; AP Photo, p. 29; © RIA Novosti/Alamy, p. 30; © Underwood & Underwood/CORBIS, p. 31; © Oasis/Photos 12/Alamy, p. 32; © Attila Kisbenedek/AFP/Getty Images, p. 34; © Sean Gallup/Getty Images, pp. 35, 36, 41; © Pete Hill/Alamy, pp. 38–39; © Aldo Pavan/Picture Contact/Alamy, p. 42; © Jan Isachsen/Art Directors & TRIP, p. 43; © Armend Nimani/AFP/Getty Images, p. 44; © David Harding/Art Directors & TRIP, p. 45; © Marek Zuk/Alamy, pp. 46, 47; © Lonely Planet/SuperStock, pp. 48–49; Barrandov Studios/The Kobal Collection, p. 52; © Richard Wareham Fotografie/Alamy, p. 54; © Peto Zvonar/Dreamstime .com, p. 56; © Hans Lippert/Imagebroker/Alamy, pp. 58–59; © J. W. Alker/ Imagebroker/Alamy, p. 60; © Tomas Hudcovic/isifa/Getty Images, p. 61; © Magdalena Rehova/Alamy, p. 63; © iStockphoto.com/Zoran Kolundzija, p. 68. Illustrations by © Laura Westlund/Independent Picture Service.

Cover: © Isifa Image Service s.r.o./Alamy.